Something's
Got to
Taste Good

Something's Got to Taste Good

The Cancer Patient's Cookbook

by Joan Fishman and Barbara Anrod
under the editorial direction of
Jory Graham

Andrews and McMeel, Inc.
A Universal Press Syndicate Company
Kansas City • New York • Washington

Library of Congress Cataloging in Publication Data

Fishman, Joan, 1954—
    Something's got to taste good.

    Bibliography
    Includes index.
    1. Cancer—Diet therapy—Recipes.
I. Anrod, Barbara, 1956—   joint author.
II. Title.
RC271.D52F57   641.5'631   80-26368
ISBN 0-8362-2102-8
ISBN 0-8362-2103-6 (pbk.)

First printing, February 1981
Second printing, September 1981

ACKNOWLEDGMENTS

The authors especially want to thank:

Beata Hayton, for giving these recipes dignity and simple elegance while at the same time simplifying their preparation, and for creating the entire herb section;

Sally Murakami, for inventive editorial assistance and unfailing patience in dealing with the hundreds of separate pieces of text that are the raw material of a cookbook;

Dolores Bradley, for tasting and sampling and giving us honest and helpful criticism.

CONTENTS

FOREWORD

Until now, no bookstore could help if you wanted a legitimate nutrition-cookbook to meet the special needs of someone who has cancer. Cookbook counters are stocked for the majority—healthy people with healthy appetites, and dieters. I have cancer, so I know the problem well.

I wrote to the few cancer centers that offered free pamphlets and booklets on cancer nutrition. Invariably, the material began with clinical descriptions of the unpleasant side effects that can occur with cancer and its treatment. Nutrition information was often repetitious and dull. Recipes (always on the last pages) were usually created for very ill people who could only take nourishment in the form of liquids. These beverages had names like "Pineapple Surprise" and I thought: *I don't want any surprises. I don't want to read about all the possible side effects of treatment I'm not even getting. I just want to find a way to enjoy good food again.* But my brain refused to signal "hungry" so I scarcely ate, even though I knew I should.

Then I met Joan Fishman, a consulting nutritionist to cancer patients at the cancer center where I was being treated. My physician insisted I see her; I simply had to stop losing weight and begin gaining weight.

Joan Fishman was the antithesis of my image of dieticians. She was inventive and flexible, and non-dogmatic about nutrition: "You don't have to eat meat if you dislike it now. You can get the same high-quality protein from chicken, eggs, or cheese."

She taught me to eat between meals: "Try snacks that provide protein and calories. At mealtime, forget the way you were brought up—if you can't face a normal dinner but can enjoy a dip with crackers, eat the dip with crackers. I'll work up some recipes for you."

Her recipes were helpful and down-to-earth. They met the basic nutritional requirements for cancer patients: high-protein, high-calorie foods that are simple and do not overwhelm. One day I printed several of her recipes in my newspaper column, which is written primarily for cancer patients and their families, and added, "Let me know if you want more recipes." Requests ran into the thousands; more than a year later they still come in.

The heads of the newspaper syndicate that distributes my column asked, "Could you write a cookbook?" I said no, not at this time; I was writing another book. "Could you plan and supervise one?" I said yes.

Joan agreed to develop the recipes. Barbara Anrod, a young writer, joined us. We produced a questionnaire for cancer patients and ran it in my column. The answers and spontaneous comments sent by readers were invaluable.*

Now we had guidelines. Our book needed to:

• Resolve the distress cancer patients feel in trying to confront three standard meals daily.

• Develop simple but appealing recipes for solid, soft, and liquid foods with flexible seasoning to compensate for the changes in taste perception that sometimes occur as a result of treatment.

• Give basic nutrition information for every recipe: calorie count and grams of protein per serving.

• Avoid an aura of "sick-room cooking," even though many recipes will meet the needs of invalided patients.

• Realize that cancer patients are not babes-in-the-woods about their clinical problems. Put the necessary clinical advice and reminders at the back of the book. Readers know how to use a table of contents and an index.

• Consider everyone who will use the book: (1) the cancer patient cooking for himself who won't cook if it means a mess of pots and pans; (2) the mother who has cancer and is gamely cooking for her family as well as for herself (she needs easy, expandable recipes); (3) the family member or friend who does the cooking but who cannot spend all day in the kitchen; (4) the cancer patient who yearns for a Big Mac and a shake.

As a cancer patient, I can assure you that Joan's recipes and Barbara's matter-of-fact approach give you an eminently helpful, reassuring book. With 170 recipes to choose from, any cancer patient should be able to regain some sense of the enjoyment of food. Best wishes and let us hear from you.

Jory Graham
A Time for Living

---

*We were surprised by the number of nutritionists who wrote asking for our findings; apparently no one has done a broad survey of the food preferences of cancer patients.

INTRODUCTION

When I was a consulting nutritionist to cancer patients in the hospital and outpatient clinic at Northwestern University Medical Center in Chicago, I was often asked, "Why do I have to eat? I'm just not hungry at all." I would say, "You need to eat because food gives you the strength to help pull you through your disease and your treatment. The protein, calories, vitamins, and minerals that food supplies help give you the energy to come to the clinic for treatment, take a drive with your family, go to work—even find the strength to get out of bed in the morning. Eating now becomes as important as your therapy. So let's see what we can do to find something that tastes good."

Though no food can cure cancer, food is vital to the well-being of every cancer patient. If your body is well nourished, then you are better able to tolerate treatment (including surgery) and resist infections. Body tissues—muscle, skin, and internal organs—are maintained and repaired with protein. That's why you'll find continuous emphasis in this book on high-protein foods. The other emphasis is on high calories, both to help your body use the protein efficiently and to keep up your weight. Every cancer patient needs almost fifty percent more protein daily than a healthy person, and at least twenty percent more calories.

I know that cancer and its treatment often result in loss of appetite and that disinterest in food underscores a sense of discouragement. But if you believe that you are going to get well, and participate in getting well, then eating regularly becomes part of your daily regimen. Sometimes considerable inner strength is required to maintain faith in the treatment your physician has ordered, but that's part of the courage needed to hold your own against your disease.

It is not necessary to be tied to three meals a day, or to the traditional meat and potatoes at your evening meal. Or, at the other extreme, to take Jello simply because it's easy to eat. If swallowing is a problem, isn't it worth knowing that one cup of the Potato Soup (page 94), a serving of the Scrambled Eggs with Cream Cheese (page 62), or a McDonald's vanilla shake each provide calories equal to the contents of an entire three-ounce package of Jello?

Well-meaning relatives or friends may encourage you to follow a particular cancer diet that they've heard will cure or arrest cancer. However, there is no scientific evidence that special diets affect cancer per se. Herbal teas, "detoxification" diets, megadose vitamin diets, grape diets, asparagus diets, and the like are nonsense nutrition and may be harmful or even detract from the benefits of your medical therapy.

If you're cooking for someone in your family who has cancer, the act of preparing food is one area where your love and concern shines through. The enjoyment of food is usually a happy and comforting activity. Yet, a seriously ill family member may reject your best efforts. When this happens, I hope you'll realize that the rejection of food is not rejection of you. Rather, it is a legitimate expression of anger or frustration over having the disease, or pain, or a very real depression. Your understanding of the total situation will help you to realize that your efforts aren't in vain.

Above all, eating is the responsibility of the one who has cancer. Though you want to encourage eating, you don't want to nag. Gentle help, patience, and small amounts of food will make a difference. As a dedicated physician told one cancer patient, "Take one day at a time; gradually each day will be easier, more comfortable, and more reassuring."

JOAN FISHMAN. R.D., M.S.

PREFACE

As a medical oncologist, I have grown accustomed to the "at intervals" nature of contemporary cancer therapy. Surgery is generally followed by a recuperative phase, radiation therapy is typically given over a "course of treatment," and cancer chemotherapy or drug treatment is often intermittent. During these intervals, nutrition may be seen as a principal or even sole "therapy" for a period of time because it is so important that the body recover from injury and the patient regain his strength.

Few things are as discouraging to an oncologist as stopping an otherwise successful program (or not giving a new program a fighting chance) because of the inadequate nutritional status of his patient. Yet, so long as we must treat the effects of cancer rather than its cause, we must depend upon the sound principles and practical advice of books such as this one to allow the therapies employed some chance for success.

I applaud the intent of this book and anticipate its adjunctive value in our fight against cancer.

> JOHN M. MERRILL, M.D.,
> *Associate Professor, Northwestern University Medical*
> *School and Cancer Center*
> August, 1980

I

A QUESTIONNAIRE AND
ITS FEEDBACK

A QUESTIONNAIRE AND ITS FEEDBACK

At the back of this book, you'll find a slightly expanded version of the questionnaire Jory ran in her newspaper column in January, 1980.* The answers, supplied by hundreds of readers, contributed directly to the kinds of recipes created for this book.

Although the survey does not qualify as a perfect statistical sample, it provided good, and even specific, guidelines to the food preferences and problems of cancer patients.

One revelation that surprised everyone was the number of cancer patients who, despite treatment, still enjoy some form of meat. Another surprise was the number of cancer patients who want highly seasoned food.

Although it wasn't specially designed to do so, the survey not only got answers—it gave answers. Some readers noted with relief that it was good to discover that their new aversion to sweets was not an aberrant happening, but stemmed from a cause (generally radiation therapy—the aversion gradually reverses itself after treatment ceases).

To the question "What do you do to alleviate nausea?" readers said they used everything from antinausea drugs like Compazine, to colas and other soft drinks. But they also ate cottage cheese and dry crackers; drank milk, milkshakes, buttermilk, and fruit juices; sucked mints; and smoked marijuana.** In our survey, half as many people are using marijuana medicinally as are using Compazine.

A considerable number of cancer patients have no problems of nausea, vomiting, or food intolerance at all—a fact that ought to be vastly reassuring to those of you who believe that the treatment of cancer always produces hideous side effects.

Jory was personally delighted to discover that her oft-repeated message—"if we have cancer, we want to be treated by cancer specialists"—is being heard. Sixty-nine percent of all who answered the questionnaire said that they were being seen by an oncologist.

Readers who have not seen the questionnaire will find it at the back of this book, and you can help us create more recipes by answering it.

---

*Similar questionnaires were also distributed to cancer patients in the clinics of university teaching hospitals in Chicago.

**This is only a partial list of the most frequent answers.

3

II

A WHOLE NEW WAY OF EATING

Anytime Snacks

Snacks almost always seem good when nothing else appeals. A handful of Trail Mix or a simple pâté spread on a small slice of French bread is not hard to eat—and might even surprise you by coaxing you into eating more of the same. Snacks also contribute to your daily calorie/protein goals. (See page 188 for how to calculate.)

The recipes in this section—dips, spreads, and snacks—are exceptionally high in calories and protein. For example: three handfuls of Trail Mix give you almost as many calories as half a pound of ground beef. Three spoonfuls of chicken liver pâté on a cracker give you as many calories and as much protein as a frankfurter. When your appetite is meager, you really must choose foods with the highest possible protein and the highest number of calories so that a little food does as big a job as possible in helping maintain your weight and your strength.

If you're cooking for yourself, the last thing you want to bother with is a lot of dishes and clean-up. The preparation of a snack calls for minimum utensils.

If you're cooking for someone in the family who has cancer, you know the person you cook for doesn't always want to make the effort to eat. Nagging is no solution—it merely upsets both of you. Snacks, several times a day, are an acceptable substitute for those times when it's too much of an effort to eat anything else.

CRUNCHY CHEESE SPREAD

One tablespoon: 85 calories, 3 grams protein.

This recipe makes from 1/2 to 3/4 cup.

1 package (3 oz.) cream cheese, softened to room temperature
1/2 Cup grated Cheddar or Colby cheese*
1/4 Cup finely chopped walnuts or almonds
1 Tb. mayonnaise
OPTIONAL:
1/2 tsp. curry powder or chili powder

Blend ingredients in a small bowl. Cover and refrigerate until ready to serve.

Or, this spread can be shaped into a log and rolled in wheat germ or finely chopped nuts. Refrigerate. When ready to serve, cut into thin slices and serve on crackers, toasted French bread, or Melba toast rounds.** Can be refrigerated up to 5 days.

---

*Cheese may be grated in a blender. Drop in small chunks of cheese, a few at a time, and flick switch on and off to grate.

**Crackers or bread will give you a few extra calories.

BEER SPREAD

Two tablespoons: 175 calories, 11 grams protein.

This recipe makes about 2 1/2 cups.

2 Cups Cheddar cheese, shredded
2 Cups Swiss cheese, shredded
1 clove garlic, minced or pressed, or, 1/4 tsp. garlic powder
1/2 tsp. dry mustard
1 tsp. Worcestershire sauce
1/2 Cup beer
OPTIONAL:
1/2 Cup chopped walnuts or pecans

Mix cheeses with garlic, mustard, and Worcestershire sauce. Beat in beer gradually until the cheese mixture is of a spreading consistency. Stir in nuts if desired. Spread on crackers or use as a dip for raw vegetables like carrots, celery, or cauliflower. Can be refrigerated, covered, up to seven days.

LIVER SAUSAGE SPREAD

One tablespoon: 45 calories, 2 grams protein.

This recipe makes about 1/2 cup.

4 oz. Braunschweiger (or other liver sausage)
1 dill pickle, minced
1/3 Cup minced celery
2 Tb. minced onion
2 Tb. pickle juice
1 tsp. lemon juice
1/2 tsp. garlic powder
Few drops of Tabasco
Salt and pepper to taste

Combine all ingredients. Mix well. Chill. Spread on crackers, bread, or toast points.

NOTE: For fresh garlic flavor, mince one clove garlic and use in place of garlic powder.

ULTIMATE CHICKEN LIVER PÂTÉ

A high-calorie pâté that's incredibly easy to prepare.

Two tablespoons: 130 calories, 3 grams protein.

This recipe makes about 2 cups.

1/2 lb. chicken livers
1/2 lb. softened butter (2 sticks)
3 or 4 Tb. brandy or bourbon, or to taste

Sauté chicken livers in 2 tablespoons of the butter just until pink in color. Do not overcook. Transfer livers to a blender; cool slightly. Add remaining butter. Add 3 tablespoons of brandy or bourbon and blend until mixture is smooth. It may be necessary to stop the blender, scrape down the sides, and start again. Add a little more liquor, if necessary, to achieve a spreadable consistency. Chill slightly and serve on crackers or party rye.

PESTO

An American version of a traditional Italian basil sauce for pasta. Also good on ripe tomato slices, or spread lightly on unsalted crackers.*

One tablespoon: 80 calories, 2 grams protein.

This recipe makes about 3/4 cup.

1/2 10 oz. package frozen chopped spinach, thawed
1/3 Cup grated Parmesan cheese
2 Tb. shelled walnuts
1 Tb. crushed, dried basil
1/2 tsp. coarse salt
1 clove garlic, crushed, or 1/2 tsp. garlic powder
1/2 Cup olive or vegetable oil
1 Tb. butter or margarine

Drain spinach, using a large spoon to press out as much liquid as possible. Put spinach in a blender container along with Parmesan cheese, nuts, seasonings, oil, and butter or margarine. Blend until smooth (about 10 seconds). It may be necessary to stop blending once or twice to scrape down sides of blender. Can be refrigerated up to three days.

---

*One Italian pesto recipe uses 2 cups fresh basil in place of spinach and omits dried basil. Another version is made with 2 cups chopped Italian (broad leaf) parsley, 2 tablespoons dried basil, and 1 cup olive oil.

11

MEXICAN BEAN DIP

One tablespoon: 45 calories, 3 grams protein.

This recipe makes about 1 cup.

1 can (15 oz.) red kidney beans, drained
1 Tb. lemon juice
1 Tb. mayonnaise
1 1/2 Tb. finely chopped fresh onion
1/4 tsp. salt
1/2 tsp. chili powder, or more to suit your taste
1 clove minced fresh garlic
1/4 Cup chopped fresh tomato
Pinch of chopped parsley for garnish

Put all the ingredients, except the parsley, into a blender. Blend for about 2 minutes or until beans are of a spreading consistency; or mash beans with a potato masher and then blend in with the rest of the ingredients. Turn into a bowl and garnish with chopped parsley. Serve with corn chips, crackers, thinly sliced French bread, or carrot sticks and celery sticks.

ARMENIAN HOMMUS DIP

Two tablespoons: 75 calories, 3 grams protein.

This recipe makes about 1 1/2 cups.

1 can (15 oz.) garbanzo beans, drained (save liquid)
2 to 4 Tb. Tahini* (sesame seed butter)
2 Tb. olive oil or vegetable oil
3 Tb. lemon juice
1 large clove garlic, minced or pressed, or 1/4 tsp. garlic powder
Salt and pepper to taste
Chopped parsley
Paprika

Put garbanzo beans into blender. Add Tahini, oil, lemon juice, and garlic. Pour in 1/4 cup of the garbanzo bean liquid and blend, with start-stop action. Add more bean liquid if necessary until mixture is smooth and the consistency of thick peanut butter. Season to taste with salt and pepper. Garnish with chopped parsley and paprika. Serve as a dip at room temperature with heated pita bread (Syrian flat bread), crackers, or fresh raw vegetables.

---

*Tahini is available in some supermarkets and most health food stores. Or, you can make a Tahini substitute as follows:

Put ¼ cup sesame seeds into blender and blend at high speed for a few seconds. Turn off blender and scrape down the sides. Repeat on-and-off process until meal is uniformly ground. Slowly add 3 tablespoons vegetable oil to sesame seed meal and blend at medium speed. The consistency should be like that of peanut butter.

GUACAMOLE

For people who crave something spicy.

Two tablespoons: 50 calories, 1/2 gram protein.

This recipe makes about 1/2 cup.

1 large avocado, ripe and soft
3 Tb. onion, minced
1 clove fresh garlic, pressed or minced
2 Tb. lemon juice
1/4 tsp. salt
1/4 tsp. pepper
A few drops Tabasco or hot sauce to taste, or one small piece of
   jalapeno pepper, seeded, rinsed, and chopped fine

Peel avocado, discard pit, and mash with a fork in a small bowl to reach
as smooth a consistency as possible. Mix in remaining ingredients.
Serve with corn chips, tortilla chips, taco chips, or crackers. Darkens
slightly if refrigerated more than one day.

To increase calories and protein:
Add 1/4 cup creamed cottage cheese, 1/4 cup chopped green olives, and 2
teaspoons mayonnaise to increase calories to 120 and grams protein to 4.

SWISS CHEESE FONDUE

One-half cup of fondue and 8 cubes of bread:
500 calories, 24 grams protein.

This recipe serves 4.

1 clove garlic
1 Cup dry white wine
1 lb. Swiss cheese, grated* (about 4 Cups)
1/4 tsp. nutmeg
1/4 tsp. salt
1/4 tsp. pepper
2 Tb. kirsch
1 loaf (1 lb.) French, Italian, or Vienna bread, cut into 1-inch cubes

Use a fondue pot or chafing dish. Rub inside of pot with cut side of garlic. Discard garlic. Pour wine into pot and heat to barely a simmer. Over low heat, add cheese, a little at a time, and stir with wooden spoon until melted. Stir in nutmeg, salt, pepper, and kirsch. Spear cubes of bread on fondue forks and dip into creamy fondue. Keep cheese warm over heating source for fondue pot or chafing dish (sterno or candle).

---

*To grate cheese easily and quickly, use a blender. Add small chunks of cheese and flick switch on and off for best results.

SESAME SEED DIP

Two tablespoons: 110 calories, 2 grams protein.

This recipe makes about 2 cups.

1 Tb. butter or margarine
1/4 Cup sesame seeds
1/4 Cup grated Parmesan cheese
1 Cup sour cream
1/2 Cup mayonnaise
1 clove of garlic, pressed
2 Tb. onion, minced
1/4 Cup cucumber, finely chopped
1/4 tsp. salt

Melt butter or margarine in small skillet. Saute' sesame seeds until lightly browned. Remove from heat and stir in Parmesan cheese. Set aside.

In a small bowl, blend sour cream and mayonnaise together. Add garlic, onion, cucumber, and salt. Stir in sesame seed mixture and mix well.

Serve with chips, crackers, or raw vegetables. It doubles as a creamy salad dressing.

SESAME CRISPS

One slice: 200 calories, 4 grams protein.

This recipe serves 2.

2 slices (1-inch thick) French or Italian bread
2 Tb. melted butter or margarine
3 Tb. grated Parmesan cheese
1 Tb. sesame seeds

Preheat oven to 400° or use a toaster oven. Brush bread with melted butter or margarine. Sprinkle liberally with Parmesan cheese and top with sesame seeds. Transfer to a baking sheet. Toast at 400° for about 5 minutes or until butter begins to bubble and cheese is melted. Serve as a snack between meals or with soup.

NOUGATS

When Joan created this recipe for one of Jory's columns, readers who tried it, loved it.

One-inch square nougat: 75 calories, 3 grams protein.

This recipe makes 12 nougats.

1/2 Cup peanut butter
1/2 Cup honey
3/4 Cup dried milk powder
1/2 Cup toasted wheat germ

Blend peanut butter and honey in a small bowl. In a separate small bowl mix milk powder and wheat germ together and gradually stir dry mixture into peanut butter-honey mixture. Turn onto waxed paper and knead until well blended. Pat down until 1/2-inch thick and cut into 1-inch squares. This can be chilled in the refrigerator for a firmer product. Store in a covered container.

TRAIL MIX

Easy combination of dried fruits, nuts, and seeds for nibbling at any time.

One-half cup: 435 calories, 13 grams protein.

This recipe makes about 3 cups.

1 Cup sunflower seeds
1/2 Cup raisins
1/2 Cup flaked coconut
1 Cup peanuts

Mix well. Store in plastic bags or airtight containers.

Try any combination of ingredients or amounts, such as cashews, walnuts, pecans, Brazil nuts, salted soy nuts* (especially high in protein: 1/4 cup gives you 140 calories, 9 grams protein), dates cut into bite-size pieces, dried apricots, dried apples, dried pears, M&M candies, chocolate chips.

---

*Also known as dry roasted soy beans.

SALTED ALMONDS

Nuts you toast and salt yourself taste better than any you can buy.

Twelve nuts: 120 calories, 2 grams protein.

This recipe makes 2 cups.

2 Tb. butter or margarine
2 Cups whole almonds, shelled
Seasoned salt to taste

Melt butter or margarine in shallow pan in a 300° oven. Add almonds; stir to coat with butter. Sprinkle with seasoned salt. Bake at 300° for 30 minutes. Stir nuts often while roasting. Store in an airtight container.

CURRIED PEANUTS

One-half cup nuts: 420 calories, 18 grams protein.

This recipe makes 2 cups.

2 Cups roasted, salted peanuts
3 tsp. curry powder

Preheat oven to 300°. Combine peanuts and curry powder in a paper bag and shake well. Spread coated peanuts in a single layer on a cookie sheet. Bake at 300° for 20 minutes. Shake pan to turn nuts once or twice while baking. Store in an airtight container.

CHEESE POPCORN

One cup: 160 calories, 5 grams protein.

This recipe makes 4 cups.

2 Tb. vegetable oil
1/2 Cup unpopped corn
Salt to taste
1/2 Cup Cheddar cheese, grated

Heat oil in a heavy skillet or saucepan. Add popcorn, cover, and place over medium-high heat. Pop, shaking continuously. Remove skillet from heat. Immediately salt to taste and sprinkle with grated cheese. Replace cover. Shake to coat evenly with cheese.

CHEESE STRAWS

One cheese straw: 50 calories, 2 grams protein.

This recipe makes about 3 dozen cheese straws.

1 stick butter or margarine (1/4 lb.)
2 Cups flour
1/4 tsp. cayenne pepper
1 clove fresh garlic, pressed, or 1/2 tsp. garlic powder
1/2 tsp. salt
4 Cups sharp Cheddar cheese, grated (about 1 lb.)
Paprika

Cream butter until soft. Add flour, cayenne pepper, garlic, salt, and cheese. Mix thoroughly to form dough. Wrap dough in waxed paper or plastic wrap and refrigerate until firm. Roll out on lightly floured waxed paper and cut into strips about 5 inches long and 1/2 inch wide. Place on a lightly greased baking sheet. Dust with paprika. Bake at 350° for about 6 minutes or until golden brown. To increase seasoning, dust before baking with cayenne pepper. Store in an airtight container.

HERBED CHEESE PRETZELS

One pretzel: 79 calories, 2 grams protein.

This recipe makes 12 pretzels.

1 Cup flour
1/2 Cup butter or margarine
3 Tb. Parmesan cheese
1 Cup sharp Cheddar cheese, shredded
1/2 tsp. each: onion, garlic powder
1/4 tsp. each: dried basil, oregano, rosemary, or 3/4 tsp. each fresh herbs
3 Tb. milk

Combine flour and butter or margarine in a medium-sized bowl. With a pastry blender (or with two knives using a cutting motion) blend until mixture forms a crumblike appearance and texture. Stir in the cheeses, herbs, and spices. Add milk. Gather mixture up into a ball with a fork or fingers. Refrigerate for 30 minutes, if necessary, for easier handling.

Preheat oven to 425°. Divide dough in half, then into 12 equal pieces. Roll each portion into ropes and then twist into pretzel shapes. Place pretzels on an ungreased cookie sheet. Bake at 425° from 12 to 15 minutes or until golden brown. Cool. Store in an airtight container.

To increase calories and protein:
One-half cup dry milk added with the cheeses will increase calories to 89 and grams protein to 3 per pretzel. If adding dry milk, add a few drops of water to mixture until you reach the desired consistency.

24

NACHOS

For people who crave food that's peppery.

One nacho: 35 calories, 1 gram protein.

This recipe makes from 20 to 25 nachos.

1 bag (5 oz.) tortilla chips
2 Cups Monterey Jack or Cheddar cheese, shredded (about 1/2 lb.)
1/2 Cup canned green chilies, rinsed, seeded, and chopped
1/2 medium onion, chopped

Preheat oven to 400°. Place tortilla chips on an ungreased baking sheet. Mix together cheese, chilies, and onion. Sprinkle 1 or 2 teaspoons of cheese mixture over each chip. Bake in a 400° oven for 5 minutes or until cheese melts. Serve piping hot.

PORK AND GINGER BALLS

This is one of Jory's favorites.

One meatball: 50 calories, 3 grams protein.

This recipe makes about 30 meatballs.

1 lb. ground pork
1 can (4 oz.) water chestnuts, drained and finely chopped
1 Tb. fresh ginger,* finely chopped, or 1 tsp. ground ginger
2 Tb. soy sauce
1 egg, beaten
1/4 Cup dry bread crumbs
1 Tb. peanut or vegetable oil

Combine pork, water chestnuts, ginger, soy sauce, egg, and bread crumbs in a medium-sized bowl and blend thoroughly. Roll into 1-inch balls. Heat the oil in a large skillet over medium heat. Add as many meatballs as will fit in the skillet without overcrowding. Fry from 5 to 8 minutes, turning often, until crisp and brown. No trace of pink should remain on the insides. Transfer meatballs to platter with slotted spoon. Serve hot or cold. These will store well for several days in the refrigerator.

NOTE: If you want to make these ahead to store in your freezer, then brown them but don't cook all the way through. Freeze in single layers on baking sheets or in shallow pans. When frozen solid, transfer to a plastic bag and seal. To reheat, place frozen pork and ginger balls on a large baking sheet, cover, and heat in a moderate (350°) oven for 15 minutes or until hot and cooked through.

---

*Fresh ginger root is available in many large supermarkets and in Chinese food markets. A small piece lasts a long time and can be frozen. Grate as needed while frozen.

MINIATURE MEAT LOGS

When everything tastes bland, try these.

One log: 82 calories, 5 grams protein.

This recipe makes 6 logs.

1 package (3 oz.) cream cheese
2 Tb. prepared horseradish or horseradish cream*
6 slices of packaged, pressed chipped beef, corned beef, pastrami,
   ham, or turkey

Blend cream cheese with horseradish. Spread on individual slices of
meat. Roll each slice and fasten with a toothpick. Chill before serving.
Cut into thirds to serve.

---

*See recipe for Horseradish Cream on page 114.

DEVILED EGGS

These are creamy, smooth, and easy to swallow.

Half a deviled egg: 75 calories, 3 grams protein.

This recipe makes 8 deviled-egg halves.

4 hard-boiled eggs
3 Tb. mayonnaise
1/4 tsp. Dijon mustard
1/4 tsp. salt
1/8 tsp. pepper
Paprika
OPTIONAL:
2 tsp. capers
1 Tb. minced parsley
1/2 tsp. Worcestershire sauce

Slice eggs in half lengthwise and slip out yolks into a small bowl. Mash yolks with a fork and blend with mayonnaise, mustard, salt, and pepper. Add optional capers, parsley, and Worcestershire sauce, if desired. Fill egg white boats with the deviled yolk mixture. Dust with paprika or top with a bit of anchovy, smoked salmon, or ham.

Mini-Meals

More substantial than snacks, lighter than conventional main dishes, mini-meals are a good source for the calories and protein a cancer patient needs to maintain energy. Like snacks, mini-meals are not a lot of work to prepare and they never create a full-scale mess in the kitchen.

If you're cooking for yourself and can't stand to look at a full plate of food, a light mini-meal may help solve that problem. Furthermore, mini-meals are loaded with calories and protein. A simple Old-Fashioned Chicken Sandwich provides 505 calories and 25 grams of protein. One bite-size Stuffed Mushroom Cap gives you 80 calories and 5 grams of protein. One serving of Welsh Rarebit gives you 450 calories and 20 grams of protein.

If you're cooking for someone in the family who has cancer, know that several mini-meal recipes make excellent breakfasts: the Apple Pancake, the Baked French Toast, and the Blender Waffles. A cancer patient often feels hungriest in the morning, so these should indeed be welcomed.

APPLE PANCAKE

One serving: 190 calories, 8 grams protein.

This recipe serves 4.

1/2 Cup flour
1 tsp. sugar
1/2 tsp. salt
3 eggs
1/2 Cup milk
2 Tb. butter or margarine
2 medium apples, peeled and thinly sliced
3 Tb. powdered sugar
1 Tb. lemon juice

Preheat oven to 400°. In a medium-sized bowl, combine flour, sugar, and salt. Beat in eggs, one at a time, with a wire whisk or wooden spoon. Slowly add milk, stirring until the batter is fairly smooth (there will be some lumps).

In a small skillet, melt butter or margarine. Sauté apple slices until they are almost soft. If the handle is ovenproof or can be wrapped in foil, then pour the batter evenly over apples in the skillet. If not, transfer apples to a 9-inch pie pan or an 8-inch shallow baking dish and add the batter. Bake at 400° for 20 minutes. Dust with powdered sugar and sprinkle with lemon juice. Serve immediately.

To increase calories:
One-half cup heavy cream substituted for 1/2 cup milk will increase calories to 235 per serving.

COTTAGE CHEESE PANCAKES

One 3-inch pancake: 80 calories, 7 grams protein.

This recipe makes from 6 to 8 pancakes.

1/3 Cup flour
3 eggs, well beaten
1 Cup small curd cottage cheese
1 Tb. butter or margarine
1/4 tsp. salt

Mix ingredients together in a large bowl until fairly smooth. To make each pancake, ladle 2 tablespoons of batter onto hot, lightly greased griddle or frying pan. Flip pancakes until golden brown on both sides.

To increase calories:
Half of a medium-sized sliced banana added to batter increases calories to 140.

One tablespoon sour cream over one pancake increases calories to 110.

POTATO PANCAKES

One 3-inch pancake: 105 calories, 2 grams protein.

This recipe makes about 9 small pancakes. Leftover cooled pancakes may be frozen and reheated in 350° oven.

3 medium potatoes, peeled and grated
1 Tb. flour
2 eggs, lightly beaten
1/2 medium onion, chopped
1/4 tsp. salt
1/8 tsp. pepper
4 Tb. oil

Combine grated potatoes, flour, eggs, onion, salt, and pepper in a large bowl and toss until well mixed. Heat oil in a large skillet. Drop about 2 tablespoons of batter onto skillet and form into flat patty with the back of a spoon. Cook about 5 minutes on one side over medium-low heat, until pancake is crisp and brown. Turn and cook other side about 5 more minutes. Repeat sequence with the rest of the batter. Keep pancakes warm in oven until ready to serve.

NOTE: Potatoes may turn brown once exposed to air, but this won't affect the taste.

To increase calories:
Two tablespoons of sour cream served with pancake will increase calories to 165.

Two tablespoons of applesauce served with pancake will increase calories to 135.

BAKED FRENCH TOAST

When you bake French toast this way, the inside of each slice is soft and fluffy and the outside oven-crisp.

One slice of French toast: 230 calories, 6 grams protein.

This recipe makes 4 slices of French toast.

2 eggs
1/4 tsp. salt
1/2 Cup milk
1 tsp. vanilla
4 slices firm, day-old bread
1/4 Cup butter, melted
OPTIONAL:
1/2 tsp. cinnamon

Preheat oven to 400°. Beat eggs, salt, milk, and vanilla together in a medium-size bowl. Add cinnamon if desired. One slice at a time, put bread into egg mixture until it's absorbed as much egg as possible. Arrange bread slices on a greased baking sheet and drizzle with the melted butter. Bake at 400° from 8 to 10 minutes on one side. Turn and bake the other side another 5 minutes or until golden brown. Serve immediately. Top with Strawberry Cream (page 115), Applesauce (page 161), or maple syrup.

TRADITIONAL FRENCH TOAST

Follow the above procedure for Baked French Toast in mixing and preparing bread slices. However, do not drizzle with butter. Instead, melt 2 tablespoons of butter in a large skillet. When butter begins to bubble, place well-soaked bread carefully into skillet and cook over low heat from 5 to 7 minutes on one side. Turn and cook another 5 minutes on the other side, until golden brown. Serve immediately.

To increase calories:
Two tablespoons of maple syrup served over a slice of French toast will increase calories to 375.

BLENDER WAFFLES

These are light and crisp—and easy to make.

One waffle: 200 calories, 8 grams protein.

This recipe makes 4 standard-sized waffles.

1 egg
1/2 Cup milk
1 Tb. vegetable oil
2 tsp. sugar
1/2 tsp. salt
2 tsp. baking powder
1 1/4 Cups flour
1/4 Cup nonfat dry milk

Combine all the ingredients in a blender container. Blend until smooth. If batter seems too thick, add more liquid milk. If too thin, add 1 to 2 tablespoons of flour. Bake on oiled, hot waffle iron. Top with Strawberry Cream Topping (page 115) or butter and warm maple syrup.

To increase calories:
Two level tablespoons of Strawberry Cream Topping on 1 waffle will increase calories to 310.

One tablespoon of butter spread on 1 waffle will increase calories to 300.

Two tablespoons of maple syrup on 1 waffle will increase calories to 300.

SAUSAGE CORN MUFFINS

One muffin: 250 calories, 7 grams protein.

This recipe makes 6 muffins.

1/2 lb. bulk pork sausage
1 Cup diced apples
1 package (8 oz.) cornmeal muffin mix
1 egg
3/4 Cup milk

Preheat oven to 400°. Fry sausage until dry and crumbly in a medium-sized skillet. Drain off excess fat. Add diced apples and cook until apples are soft. Prepare cornmeal mix, adding the egg and milk as directed on the package. Stir in sausage and apples. Spoon batter into a greased 6-cup muffin tin. Bake at 400° for 20 minutes. Remove from oven and let muffins cool in tin for 5 minutes. Muffins taste best when served warm with butter or apple butter.

To increase calories:
Two tablespoons of butter spread on 1 muffin will increase calories to 450.

Two tablespoons of apple butter spread on 1 muffin will increase calories to 316.

WELSH RAREBIT

One serving (with 1 slice of bread or half of an English muffin):
450 calories, 20 grams protein.

This recipe serves 3.

1/2 Cup beer, warmed to room temperature
1 egg yolk
1/2 tsp. Worcestershire sauce
2 Tb. butter or margarine
1/4 tsp. dry mustard
Pinch of cayenne pepper
2 Cups grated Cheddar cheese
Buttered toast or toasted English muffins

Beat beer, egg yolk, and Worcestershire sauce together and set aside.

Melt butter or margarine in the top of a double boiler. Stir in mustard and cayenne. Add cheese, 1/4 cup at a time, to butter mixture, stirring constantly with a wooden spoon. When cheese begins to form a thick mass, add a little of the beer and egg mixture. Stirring constantly, alternately add the rest of the cheese and the beer mixture. Continue stirring, over low heat, for about 10 minutes or until mixture is hot and smooth.

Spoon over toast or muffins and serve at once.

KUGEL

One serving: 305 calories, 12 grams protein.

This recipe serves 4.

1/2 lb. broad egg noodles
1 Cup sour cream
1 Cup small curd cottage cheese
1/2 Cup milk
1/2 tsp. salt
2 Tb. sugar
1/4 Cup toasted wheat germ or bread crumbs
3 Tb. butter or margarine

Preheat oven to 375°. Cook egg noodles according to package directions. Drain. Mix noodles with sour cream, cottage cheese, milk, salt, and sugar. Place in a shallow, greased 2-quart casserole or oven-proof dish. Sprinkle with toasted wheat germ or bread crumbs. Dot the top liberally with butter or margarine. Bake at 375° for 50 minutes.

SWEET KUGEL

One serving: 345 calories, 12 grams protein.

Follow the above procedure for Kugel, but add 1/2-cup drained, crushed pineapple and 1/4-cup raisins to the noodle mixture. Sprinkle the top with cinnamon.

RICE PILAF

One-half cup: 280 calories, 8 grams protein.

This recipe serves 4.

3 Tb. olive oil or margarine
1 Cup rice, uncooked
1/2 tsp. salt
1/4 tsp. freshly ground pepper
2 Cups beef or chicken broth
OPTIONAL:
1 Cup chopped fresh or canned mushrooms

Heat oil or melt margarine in medium-sized saucepan. Add rice and brown, stirring constantly, for 3 minutes. Add salt, pepper, broth, and mushrooms (if desired). Cover and simmer for 20 minutes. When done, lightly fluff rice with a fork. This can be served as a side dish with fish, poultry, or meat.

FRIED RICE

Use any leftover meats or vegetables in this dish.

One cup fried rice: 400 calories, 16 grams protein.

This recipe serves 4.

4 Tb. oil
3 Cups cooked rice
1 Cup finely diced meat—ham, beef, shrimp, chicken, or crumbled bacon
1/4 Cup green pepper, diced
1/4 Cup green onions, sliced
3 eggs, well beaten
1 to 2 Tb. good soy sauce to taste

Heat oil in medium-sized skillet or wok. Brown cooked rice for about 3 minutes. Add meat, green pepper, and onion and any leftover vegetables you desire. Continue cooking, stirring occasionally to avoid burning, for another 3 minutes. Push the rice to the sides of skillet to form a well in the middle. Pour eggs into the well and let set for a minute. Lightly scramble, then gently mix in with rice. Add soy sauce and serve.

EGG FOO YUNG

Traditionally this is a dish that uses leftovers. Almost any vegetables or meats can be used, as long as they are shredded or cut into small chunks so they can bind with the eggs and form a patty.

One patty: 175 calories, 18 grams protein.

This recipe makes from 4 to 6 patties.

4 eggs, slightly beaten
1 Cup diced chicken or any leftover cooked meat or shrimp
1/4 Cup finely chopped celery
1/4 Cup minced green onion
1/4 Cup chopped mushrooms
1/2 Cup bean sprouts (if canned, drain well)
2 tsp. good soy sauce
1 clove fresh garlic, minced, or 1/4 tsp. garlic powder
Vegetable oil for frying
OPTIONAL:
1 10 1/2 oz. can chicken gravy
2 tsp. soy sauce

Blend beaten eggs with meat and vegetables. Add soy sauce and garlic. For each patty, pour out about 1/4-cup of the mixture onto a hot, lightly greased skillet. Brown evenly on both sides. Heat chicken gravy mixed with 2 teaspoons soy sauce and spoon over each patty. Serve immediately. Every tablespoon of gravy adds 15 calories.

MEAT EMPANADAS

One meat empanada: 200 calories, 8 grams protein.

This recipe makes 9 empanadas.

FILLING:
1/2 lb. ground beef
2 Tb. paprika
1/2 Cup chopped onion
1/4 tsp. salt
1/8 tsp. pepper
1/2 tsp. cinnamon
2 hard-boiled eggs, chopped
1 Tb. stuffed green olives, chopped
2 Tb. raisins
CRUST:
Use a packaged puff pastry dough,* thawed, or packaged crescent roll dough.

FILLING: Sprinkle paprika over beef. Brown beef in a medium-sized skillet. Add onions and saute until soft. Add seasonings and remaining ingredients. Remove from heat and set aside.

CRUST: Preheat oven to 350°. Cut the sheet of puff pastry dough into 9 3-inch squares. Place 1 1/2 tablespoons of filling in the middle of each square and fold over to make a triangle. Press edges together with tines of fork to seal. Place on an ungreased cookie sheet and bake at 350° for 20 minutes or until golden brown. (If using crescent roll dough, bake at 350° for 10 minutes.) Empanadas, baked or unbaked, can be frozen up to one month.

---

*Can be found in the frozen-foods section of your grocery store.

RICOTTA GNOCCHI

This is a light Italian cheese dumpling.

One gnocchi: 45 calories, 3 grams protein.

This recipe makes 12 gnocchi.

1/4 Cup ricotta cheese*
2 egg yolks
3/4 Cup Parmesan cheese
1/4 Cup flour
1 tsp. salt
1/2 tsp. fresh ground pepper
1/2 tsp. nutmeg

Stir ricotta cheese, egg yolks, 1/2-cup of the Parmesan cheese, flour, and seasonings together in medium-sized bowl. This mixture can be prepared ahead of time, refrigerated, and formed into dumplings later. Bring 8 cups of lightly salted water to a boil. Meanwhile spread about 1/2-cup flour on a dinner plate. Form 1 tablespoon of cheese mixture into a ball and roll in flour. Drop the first ball into the rapidly boiling water as a test. It should retain its shape and rise to the top, cooked, after about 2 minutes. If the ball should fall apart, add 1 or 2 more teaspoons of flour to the raw dough. Before making the rest of the dumplings, grease a small ovenproof serving or baking dish with about 1 tablespoon of butter. Proceed to form, flour, and cook the rest of the dumplings as described above. As they rise to the top, fish them out of the water with a slotted spoon and place them in the buttered dish. Sprinkle with the remaining Parmesan cheese and serve immediately. If you want to make gnocchi ahead of time, boil, place in buttered dish, cover with foil, and refrigerate—they will keep about a day. Before serving, sprinkle with cheese and heat, covered, in a 350° oven for 5 minutes.

---

*If you can't find ricotta cheese, you can substitute cottage cheese. Drain well in a colander and transfer to a blender container. Blend until smooth, about 3 minutes.

STUFFED MUSHROOM CAPS

Yields high calories in bite sizes.

One large mushroom cap: 80 calories, 5 grams protein.

This recipe makes 10 or 12 stuffed mushroom caps.

10 to 12 large mushroom caps, stems removed
10 to 12 mushroom stems, finely chopped
1/2 lb. lean ground beef
2 Tb. bread crumbs
1 tsp. salt
1/2 tsp. fresh ground pepper
1/2 tsp. summer savory
A few drops of Worcestershire sauce to moisten
4 Tb. butter or margarine, melted

Mix mushroom stems, beef, bread crumbs, and seasonings well with wet hands. Add a few drops Worcestershire sauce to moisten stuffing.

Lavishly brush mushroom caps inside and out with melted butter or margarine. Broil rounded-side-up for 2 or 3 minutes. Turn over and fill each mushroom cap with beef, mounding slightly. Brush the tops with remaining melted butter or margarine. Place under broiler for 7 to 10 minutes or until meat is browned and mushrooms are juicy.

QUICK STUFFED MUSHROOM CAPS

One large mushroom cap: 50 calories, 2 grams protein.

Instead of using the stuffing above, fill each mushroom cap with a spoonful of barely browned pork sausage. You'll need approximately 1/2 lb. bulk ground pork sausage to fill 10 to 12 large mushroom caps. Broil 5 to 6 minutes.

MUSHROOMS À LA RUSSE

One serving: 220 calories, 5 grams protein.

This recipe serves 4.

3 Tb. butter or margarine
1 lb. fresh mushrooms, sliced
1 small onion, finely chopped
Pepper to taste
1/2 tsp. salt
2 tsp. flour
1 Cup sour cream
Dash Worcestershire sauce

Heat butter in a medium-sized skillet. Add mushrooms and onion. Sauté until almost soft. Season with pepper and salt and sprinkle with flour. Stir until well mixed. Lower heat, cover, and simmer a few minutes. Stir in sour cream, a little at a time. Do not allow mixture to boil. Add a dash of Worcestershire sauce. Serve alone or on toast or a baked potato to increase the calories.

DEVILED FRANKFURTERS

Each 2-inch deviled frank: 60 calories, 2 grams protein.

This recipe makes 2 dozen deviled franks.

8 frankfurters
2 Tb. butter
1/2 tsp. dry mustard
3 Tb. chili sauce
2 Tb. sour cream
1/4 tsp. Worcestershire sauce

Boil franks as usual. Cut each one into 3 pieces. Melt butter in medium-sized saucepan. Add dry mustard and stir well. Add chili sauce, sour cream, and Worcestershire sauce. Heat thoroughly, but do not allow to boil. When sauce is hot, add franks. Continue cooking another 3 or 4 minutes, until franks are heated through. Serve immediately. Skewer with a toothpick to eat.

OLD-FASHIONED CHICKEN SANDWICH

This is the kind of chicken sandwich you can't get in most restaurants these days.

One chicken sandwich: 505 calories, 25 grams protein.

This recipe serves 1.

2 slices whole wheat bread
2 Tb. mayonnaise or butter
Fresh green lettuce leaf
3 oz. poached breast of chicken, sliced against the grain*

Spread bread with mayonnaise or butter. Arrange lettuce leaf on one slice and neatly tuck chicken slices on top. Sprinkle with a little salt, if desired.

---

*To prepare Poached Chicken:
Clean and truss a small chicken. Place in tightly covered pot with just enough water to lap against lower third of chicken. Bring water to a boil and lower heat immediately to a simmer. After 5 minutes, skim the grease. Now add a little salt, freshly ground pepper, a small, thinly-sliced onion, a carrot cut into small pieces, some crumbled dried celery leaves, and some dried thyme. Cook gently one hour or more until chicken is loose on the bones. Remove and cool. Cut away from bones and refrigerate until ready to use. Chicken will keep several days.

Strain the leftover stock into a bowl or jar, cover, and refrigerate to use as soup or chicken soup stock.

46

DEEP-DISH PIZZA

One serving: 220 calories, 7 grams protein.

This recipe serves 4.

3 Cups Bisquick mix
1/3 Cup powdered milk
3/4 Cup water
1 can (8 oz.) pizza sauce or 1 can (8 oz.) tomato sauce
1 tsp. oregano
1/2 medium-sized green pepper, cut into julienne strips
8 to 10 fresh mushrooms, sliced, or 1 can (4 oz.) sliced mushrooms
1 Cup (4 oz.) mozzarella cheese, shredded
OPTIONAL:
Top pizza with sausage, pepperoni, Canadian bacon, onion, anchovies—
  the combinations are almost endless.

Preheat oven to 425°. Lightly grease a 9 x 9 x 2-inch pan. Mix Bisquick, powdered milk, and water together to form a soft dough. With well-floured hands, shape dough into pan and push up on the sides to form a rim. Spoon pizza or tomato sauce evenly over the dough. Sprinkle with oregano and top with peppers, mushrooms, cheese, and any other toppings of your choice. Bake at 425° for 20 minutes or until crust is a golden brown.

THIN CRUST PIZZA

One serving: 200 calories, 5 grams protein.

This recipe serves 4.

Follow above procedure for Deep-Dish Pizza, but substitute a frozen 10-inch pizza shell for dough and bake on a round, 10-inch pizza pan instead of in a baking pan.

PIZZA BREAD

One serving: 200 calories, 5 grams protein.

This recipe serves 4.

Follow the Deep-Dish Pizza recipe for tomato sauce and toppings. Split one long loaf (14 to 16 inches) of French or Italian bread lengthwise. Place both halves on a foil-lined cookie sheet, split-side up. Top with sauce, cheese, and other toppings.

Place the pizza bread under the broiler for 5 to 7 minutes, or until cheese begins to bubble.

Danish Open-Faced Sandwiches

Danish sandwiches are appealing—breadcrusts are trimmed and the sandwiches are cut into neat thirds or quarters. Considering the fact that Danish sandwiches are made on single slices of bread, they are surprisingly nutritious, for the bread is often spread with nicely caloric sweet (unsalted) butter, and each sandwich is built from this base.

If you're cooking for yourself, think of the ease of making the simple Avocado and Cream Cheese Sandwich and getting 400 calories plus 7 grams of protein with almost no effort.

If you're cooking for someone in your family who has cancer but you must be away from home much of the day, put a pretty Danish sandwich on a plate in the refrigerator. It is more likely to tempt a cancer patient to eat than hot dishes which require preparation and pots and pans.

ROAST BEEF OPEN-FACED SANDWICH

One sandwich: 265 calories, 9 grams protein.

This recipe makes 1 open-faced sandwich.

1 slice of whole wheat bread, trimmed of its crust, and spread with
  sweet butter
1 or 2 thin slices of roast beef
1 Tb. horseradish cream*

Top buttered bread with roast beef. Slice into thirds and decorate
each piece with a little horseradish cream. Serve with fresh radishes.

---

*See page 114 for Horseradish Cream.

HAM AND EGG OPEN-FACED SANDWICH

One sandwich: 280 calories, 8 grams protein.

This recipe makes 1 open-faced sandwich.

3 to 4 slices of hard-boiled egg
1 slice of buttered rye bread, trimmed of its crust
1 to 2 thin slices of ham
OPTIONAL:
Freshly ground pepper

Arrange egg slices on the buttered slice of rye. Top with ham and a little pepper. Cut sandwich into thirds and serve with 2 or 3 green pepper rings.

SHRIMP OPEN-FACED SANDWICH

One sandwich: 75 calories, 2 grams protein.

This recipe makes 1 open-faced sandwich.

2 Tb. tiny canned shrimp, drained and rinsed
1 Tb. mayonnaise*
1 tsp. mustard
A few drops of lemon juice
Minced parsley
1 slice rye bread, trimmed of its crust
OPTIONAL:
Freshly ground pepper

Mix shrimp with mayonnaise, mustard, and lemon juice. Add a little minced parsley and a little pepper, if desired. Spread on bread. Cut sandwich into thirds and serve with celery sticks.

---

*See page 113 for Easy Blender Mayonnaise. Your sandwich will taste much fresher if you use homemade, rather than prepared, mayonnaise.

SARDINE OPEN-FACED SANDWICH

One sandwich: 225 calories, 8 grams protein.

This recipe makes 1 open-faced sandwich.

1 slice of rye bread, trimmed of its crust, and spread with sweet butter,
  mustard, or mayonnaise
3 to 4 slices of a ripe tomato
2 sardines
Fresh lemon wedge

Arrange tomato slices on bread. Top with sardines. Squeeze fresh
lemon over sardines. Cut sandwich in half on the diagonal.

SWISS CHEESE OPEN-FACED SANDWICH

One sandwich: 275 calories, 9 grams protein.

This recipe makes 1 open-faced sandwich.

1 slice dark rye or pumpernickel, trimmed of its crust, and spread with
 sweet butter
1 slice of Swiss cheese
1 tsp. chives (to taste)

Sprinkle chives over buttered bread and top with cheese. Cut into
thirds and serve with carrot sticks.

AVOCADO AND CREAM CHEESE
OPEN-FACED SANDWICH

One sandwich: 400 calories, 7 grams protein.

This recipe makes 1 open-faced sandwich.

3 Tb. softened cream cheese
3 to 4 slices fresh, ripe avocado
1 slice whole wheat bread, trimmed of its crust
OPTIONAL:
Pepper to taste
Lemon to taste

Mash cream cheese with avocado. Season to taste with pepper and lemon, if desired. Spread over bread. Cut into thirds and serve with pimiento-stuffed olives.

CREAM CHEESE AND OLIVE
OPEN-FACED SANDWICH

One sandwich: 240 calories, 5 grams protein.

This recipe makes 1 open-faced sandwich.

1 slice whole wheat bread, trimmed of its crust
3 Tb. softened cream cheese
3 Tb. sliced pimiento-stuffed olives
1/2 tsp. chives

Spread cream cheese on bread. Decorate with olive slices and chives.
Cut bread in half and serve with 2 or 3 slices of cooked, pickled beets.

CREAM CHEESE AND STRAWBERRY JAM
OPEN-FACED SANDWICH

One sandwich: 225 calories, 2 grams protein.

This recipe makes 1 open-faced sandwich.

1 slice of whole wheat bread, trimmed of its crust
2 Tb. of softened cream cheese
1 Tb. strawberry jam

Spread cream cheese on bread, top with strawberry jam. Cut slices into quarters and serve with hot chocolate or tea.

PEANUT BUTTER OPEN-FACED SANDWICH

One sandwich: 410 calories, 14 grams protein.

This recipe makes 1 open-faced sandwich.

1 slice of whole wheat or limpa* bread, trimmed of its crust, and
    buttered
3 Tb. peanut butter
1 Tb. bacon bits
OPTIONAL:
Chutney

Spread bread with peanut butter, bacon bits, and a little chutney (if desired). Slice into thirds and serve with ripe olives.

---

*See page 78 for Swedish Limpa Bread.

Cheese and Egg Dishes

When meat, fish, and poultry no longer taste good, egg and cheese dishes, with equally high protein, usually hold their own. Eggs and cheese are soft and moist—and rarely difficult to swallow.

Many people worry about the cholesterol content of eggs. But, for a cancer patient, the benefits gained from eating eggs—if eggs are the only high-protein foods that taste good—outweigh the effects of high cholesterol. A cancer patient whose blood is being analyzed regularly does not need to worry because any significant rise in the cholesterol level will be noted. Double-check with your doctor if you have any doubts or questions.

It's interesting to note that a cancer patient often welcomes a genuine meal in the morning. This is all to the good because a reasonably hearty first-meal-of-the-day creates energy that carries over into the rest of the day. Should cancer patients lose interest in food as the day progresses, snacks can meet the rest of their nutritional needs.

If you're cooking for yourself, you'll like these egg and cheese recipes because they are so easy to prepare, so easy to eat.

If you're cooking for someone in the family who has cancer, and who says that meat tastes bitter, chicken tastes dull, and fish tastes awful, switch to cheese and egg recipes. Drug treatment doesn't seem to alter their fresh taste.

BAKED EGG IN CREAM

One baked egg: 200 calories, 8 grams protein.

This recipe serves 1.

1/4 Cup cream
1/2 tsp. Worcestershire sauce or 1/4 tsp. dry mustard
1 drop Tabasco sauce
1 egg

Preheat oven to 500°. Liberally butter a small ovenproof dish or custard cup. Add cream, Worcestershire sauce (or dry mustard), and Tabasco sauce. Beat with a fork to blend thoroughly. Bake at 500° for about 4 minutes or until cream boils rapidly. Remove from oven and turn off oven. Carefully break egg into the dish. Return to hot oven from 4 to 6 minutes, depending on how firm you like your egg yolk. Serve immediately with a toasted English muffin or egg bagel. One English muffin provides 130 calories; one egg bagel provides 140 calories.

EGGS IN CHEESE SAUCE

One serving: 465 calories, 20 grams protein.

This recipe serves 2.

2 hard-boiled eggs, sliced
2 slices whole wheat toast
1 Cup Basic Cheese Sauce (page 108)
Pinch cayenne pepper
Pinch nutmeg

Arrange egg slices on toast. Transfer to a baking sheet or shallow pan. Pour hot cheese sauce over eggs. Sprinkle lightly with pepper and nutmeg to taste. Place under the broiler for 2 or 3 minutes or until cheese is lightly browned and bubbly.

NOTE: To prevent the rubbery texture that comes from hard boiling, cover eggs in cold water in saucepan. Bring the water to a boil. Remove pan from heat immediately. Put lid on pan. Let eggs sit 15 to 20 minutes. Plunge into cold water and peel as soon as they are cool enough to handle. Instant peeling keeps the yolks from blackening.

SCRAMBLED EGGS WITH CREAM CHEESE

One serving: 450 calories, 18 grams protein.

This recipe serves 2.

4 eggs
2 Tb. milk
2 Tb. butter or margarine
3 oz. cream cheese, cut into small cubes
8 to 10 green olives, sliced

Beat eggs and milk together in a small bowl. Melt butter in a medium-sized skillet over medium heat. When bubbly, add egg mixture. Stir gently with a wooden spoon to scramble. When eggs have almost set, add cream cheese and allow it to melt into eggs. Stir in olives. Salt and pepper eggs and serve immediately.

EGGS RANCHEROS

This is a traditional Spanish or Latin American dish. The eggs can be baked in the sauce or poached first and smothered in sauce afterward.

One egg ranchero: 150 calories, 8 grams protein.
One tortilla: 63 calories, 1 gram protein.

This recipe makes 4 eggs rancheros.

2 Tb. olive or vegetable oil
1 clove garlic, crushed
1/2 medium green pepper, chopped
2 Cups chopped fresh tomatoes or 1 can (1 lb.) chopped tomatoes with liquid
1/2 tsp. salt
1/4 tsp. freshly ground pepper
2 tsp. chili powder
1/4 tsp. oregano
4 eggs
Tortillas
OPTIONAL:
3 Tb. grated Cheddar cheese

Heat oil in a medium-sized skillet. Sauté garlic until soft. Remove garlic and discard. Sauté green pepper for 3 to 4 minutes. Add tomatoes and seasonings. Simmer, covered, until sauce is slightly thickened and well blended. At this point, poach 4 eggs in a separate pan* or carefully break eggs into hot, simmering tomato sauce. Cover and cook for 5 minutes or until eggs are set. Remove to serving plate and sprinkle each egg with a little grated Cheddar cheese if you wish. If you poach eggs separately, spoon sauce over eggs. Serve with warm tortillas.

---

*To poach eggs, fill a shallow saucepan or skillet with enough water to just cover the eggs. Add 1 tablespoon vinegar and a pinch of salt to the water. Bring to a rapid boil. Carefully break eggs into boiling water and cook until eggs are set, about 5 minutes. Remove with a slotted spoon to a serving platter.

OPEN-FACED OMELET (FRITTATA)

One serving: 225 calories, 13 grams protein.

This recipe serves 4.

3 Tb. butter or margarine
1 small onion, chopped, or 2 Tb. chopped fresh parsley
10 fresh mushrooms, sliced, or 1 can (4 oz.) sliced mushrooms
6 eggs
1/2 tsp. salt
1/4 tsp. pepper
1/3 Cup Parmesan cheese
1/4 tsp. basil (dried) or 1/2 tsp. fresh basil
1/8 tsp. nutmeg

In a medium-sized skillet, melt butter or margarine. Lightly sauté onion (or parsley). Add sliced mushrooms and sauté another five minutes over medium heat.

In a small bowl, beat eggs lightly with salt and pepper. Add to skillet. Lower heat and cook until eggs are set, about 8 to 10 minutes.

Sprinkle cheese over top, along with basil and nutmeg. Place under broiler for a few minutes until cheese is melted. Cut into wedges. Serve hot or slightly warm.

WESTERN OMELET

One serving: 430 calories, 23 grams protein.

This recipe serves 2.

3 Tb. butter or margarine
1/3 Cup onion, finely chopped
1/3 Cup green pepper, finely chopped
2 slices ham, chopped, (2 oz.)
4 eggs, slightly beaten
1/2 tsp. salt
1/4 tsp. freshly ground pepper
2 slices buttered toast

Melt butter or margarine in a medium-sized skillet. Add onion, green pepper, and ham. Cook until vegetables are soft. Pour eggs over vegetables and ham; add salt and pepper. Cook over low heat until eggs are set. Carefully turn with a spatula and brown the other side. Divide omelet in half. Place each half on a piece of buttered toast. Serve immediately.

CHEESE BLINTZES

One cheese blintz: 125 calories, 10 grams protein.

This recipe makes 12 to 14 cheese blintzes.

FILLING:
1 lb. farmer's cheese or dry curd cottage cheese
1 egg
1 Tb. sugar
1 Tb. softened butter
A pinch of salt
BATTER:
2 eggs
1/2 tsp. salt
1 tsp. sugar
1 Cup milk
1 Tb. melted butter
1 Cup flour, sifted with 1/4 tsp. baking powder
TOPPING:
Sour cream, fresh blueberries or strawberries

FILLING: Press farmer's cheese or cottage cheese through a fine strainer. Mix with egg, sugar, butter, and salt in a medium-sized bowl. Set aside until ready to use.

BATTER: Beat eggs until light and foamy in a large bowl. Add salt, sugar, milk, melted butter, and flour sifted with baking powder. Beat until smooth. Drop batter, 2 tablespoons at a time, onto a well-greased 5-inch skillet over medium heat. Tip skillet so batter spreads evenly and thinly over entire pan. Pour off any excess. Cook on one side until top is dry and starts to blister. Transfer to a flat board. Fill with 1 tablespoon of filling. Roll up and tuck in ends. Refrigerate until ready to serve or freeze. When ready to serve, brush tops with melted butter and bake at 400° for 30 minutes. Top with sour cream, fresh blueberries or strawberries.

MUSHROOM QUICHE

One serving: 255 calories, 10 grams protein.

This recipe serves 8.

1/2 lb. fresh mushrooms, sliced
2 Tb. onion, finely chopped
2 Tb. butter or margarine
9-inch frozen, deep-dish pie crust, partially baked for ten minutes
    in a hot (400°) oven
1 1/3 Cups Swiss cheese, finely shredded*
3 eggs
1 1/2 Cups half & half
Salt and freshly ground pepper to taste
Generous pinch of freshly grated nutmeg or 2 shakes of
    ground nutmeg

Preheat oven to 400°

Saute mushrooms and onion in butter or margarine until liquid cooks away. Place in pie crust.

Sprinkle Swiss cheese over mushrooms and onion.

In a separate bowl, beat eggs, half & half, salt, pepper, and nutmeg until well blended. Pour over the cheese and mushrooms in pie shell. Bake at 400° for 20 minutes or until knife inserted into center of quiche comes out clean.

---

*If presliced Swiss cheese is used, cut into thin strips (julienne).

CHEESE SOUFFLÉ

This recipe serves 4.

1/3 Cup vegetable oil
2/3 Cup flour
1 Cup milk
1 tsp. salt
1 tsp. pepper
4 eggs, separated
2 Cups (16 oz.) large curd cottage cheese
2/3 Cup Swiss cheese, grated
OPTIONAL:
1 tsp. curry powder
2 Tb. lemon juice

Preheat oven to 300°. Heat oil in a medium-sized saucepan. Stir in flour. Gradually add milk, stirring constantly. Allow mixture to thicken slightly. Remove from heat. Add salt, pepper, well-beaten egg yolks, cottage cheese, Swiss cheese, curry powder, and lemon juice. Mix thoroughly. Beat egg whites until stiff peaks form and gently fold into cheese mixture. Carefully transfer to 1 1/2 or 2-quart greased baking dish, casserole, or soufflé dish. Bake at 300° for 1 hour. Do *not* open oven while soufflé is baking or it will probably fall. Serve immediately.

POTATO SOUFFLE'

One serving: 350 calories, 15 grams protein.

This recipe serves 4.

8 medium-sized potatoes, peeled and quartered
3/4 Cup milk
1 1/2 tsp. salt
5 eggs, separated
2 Tb. butter
1 tsp. nutmeg

Preheat oven to 375°. Boil potatoes until soft. Drain and transfer to a large mixing bowl. Gradually mix in milk, with electric mixer set at low speed. Finish up at medium speed and blend until smooth. Add salt. In a separate, smaller mixing bowl, beat egg whites until stiff. Blend egg yolks into potato mixture. Carefully fold in stiff egg whites. Transfer to a casserole or souffle' dish. Dot the top with butter and sprinkle with nutmeg. Bake at 375° for 20 to 25 minutes or until the top is a light golden-brown. Serve immediately.

BEAN AND CHEESE TORTILLA

A soft tortilla with good nutrition.

One serving: 485 calories, 22 grams protein.

This recipe serves 4.

1 medium onion, chopped
1 green pepper, chopped
2 Tb. oil
1 can (15 oz.) kidney beans, drained
1 can (15 oz.) tomato sauce
1/2 Cup beef bouillon
1 or 2 Tb. chili powder (to taste)
1 tsp. salt
1/2 tsp. pepper
4 corn or flour tortillas
1 Cup cottage cheese
1/2 to 3/4 Cup Monterey Jack or Cheddar cheese, grated
6 to 8 black olives, chopped

Sauté onion and green pepper in oil until soft. Blend beans in a blender for about 2 minutes or mash beans with a potato masher. Add to onion and green pepper. Add tomato sauce, bouillon, and spices. Simmer over low heat for about 15 minutes. Meanwhile, preheat oven to 350°.

When sauce is ready, spoon a few tablespoons into a 3-quart casserole or ovenproof baking dish to cover bottom. Place a tortilla over sauce. Spread with 3 tablespoons of cottage cheese, 2 tablespoons grated cheese, and 1/4 cup sauce. Repeat this sequence until all the ingredients are used. End with a sprinkle of cheese over last tortilla. Garnish with chopped black olives.

Bake at 350° for about 20 or 25 minutes, until cheese is bubbly. Cut into wedges and serve.

CHEESE PUFFS

One cheese puff: 275 calories, 6 grams protein.

This recipe makes 2 cheese puffs.

2 slices of bread, any kind
1 package (3 oz.) cream cheese
1 egg yolk
1 tsp. mayonnaise
1 tsp. grated or minced onion

Lightly toast bread. Cream remaining ingredients and spread on toast. Broil under a hot broiler for about 2 minutes or until slightly browned.

71

HERBED COTTAGE CHEESE

Two tablespoons: 75 calories, 4 grams protein.

This recipe makes half a cup.

1/2 Cup cottage cheese
3 Tb. cream cheese, softened at room temperature
1 tsp. butter or margarine
Generous Tb. of fresh chopped parsley and fresh chopped dill or 1/2 Tb. dried
    dill weed—or other fresh herbs as available
1/8 tsp. freshly ground pepper
1/4 tsp. salt

Blend all ingredients together well. Serve as a dip with crackers, on thin slices of pumpernickel bread, or as a topping on thick slices of fresh tomato.

EGG SALAD

One serving: 345 calories, 14 grams protein.

This recipe serves 4.

2 Tb. lemon juice
2 Tb. chives, finely chopped
1 Tb. fresh dill, chopped, or 1 1/2 tsp. dried dill, crumbled
1 Tb. fresh basil or 1/2 tsp. summer savory, finely chopped
1/2 Cup mayonnaise
1/2 tsp. salt
1/4 tsp. freshly ground pepper
8 hard-boiled eggs, finely chopped

Combine lemon juice, chives, dill, fresh basil or summer savory, mayonnaise, salt, and pepper in a mixing or salad bowl. Blend well. Add diced eggs and toss gently to mix. Serve on a bed of lettuce or as a topping on thick slices of fresh tomato.

Breads and Muffins

When a cancer patient feels "spacey" or exhausted, a simple piece of bread and butter can restore a sense of well-being faster than other high-protein or high-fat foods. The reason for this is that the human body uses carbohydrates (which bread supplies) more quickly than it does proteins or fats.

If you're cooking for yourself, it's good to know that only one of these bread doughs requires kneading or punching down. The recipe for Swedish Limpa Bread—usually a complicated bread—is presented here as a cool-rising bread. The Beer Bread, which tastes very much like a yeast bread, is even simpler to make. And muffins and popovers rise in the oven during baking.

If you're cooking for someone in the family who has cancer, these recipes offer a good change of pace from supermarket breads. Some are eggy; some are almost cakelike in texture; some are fairly dense. Try serving them with sweet butter—its fresh, light taste is often more appealing than salted butter or margarine.

WHOLE WHEAT RAISIN BREAD

One slice: 130 calories, 5 grams protein.

This recipe makes 1 loaf of 16 slices.

2 Cups whole wheat flour
1/2 Cup soy flour
1/2 Cup nonfat dry milk
1 tsp. baking soda
1 tsp. baking powder
1/4 Cup brown sugar
2 Cups sour milk*
1 Cup raisins

Preheat oven to 350°. Combine flours, dry milk, baking soda, baking powder, and brown sugar in a large mixing bowl. Add sour milk and mix until well moistened. Stir in the raisins. Turn into a well-greased 8 1/2 x 4 1/2 x 2 1/2-inch loaf pan.

Bake at 350° for 50 to 60 minutes or until the top is brown. Turn out on a wire rack to cool.

*To make sour milk, mix 2 cups of milk with 2 teaspoons of lemon juice or vinegar.

BEER BREAD

This is a simple yeastlike bread.

One slice: 160 calories, 4 grams protein.

This recipe makes 1 loaf of 12 slices.

3 Cups self-rising flour*
3 Tb. sugar
1/4 Cup dry powdered milk
1 egg
1 can (12 oz.) warm beer
2 Tb. butter or margarine, melted

Mix flour, sugar, and powdered milk together in a large bowl. Add egg and beer and mix until dough is soft and spongy. Turn dough into a greased 8 1/2 x 4 1/2 x 2 1/2-inch loaf pan. Let dough rest 10 minutes. Preheat oven to 400°. Bake at 400° for 30 minutes. Brush the top with melted butter and return to 400° oven for an additional 30 minutes.

SWEET BEER BREAD

One slice: 210 calories, 5 grams protein.

Follow the above procedure for Beer Bread, but add 1/2 cup raisins and 1/2 cup of chopped nuts (any kind) to the dry ingredients.

CHEESE BEER BRÉAD

One slice: 200 calories, 6 grams protein.

Follow the procedure for beer bread, but add 1 cup shredded cheddar cheese along with the egg and beer.

HERB-BLEND BEER BREAD

One slice: 160 calories, 4 grams protein.

Follow procedure on the preceding page for Beer Bread, but add 1/2 teaspoon of oregano, 1/2 teaspoon of thyme, and 1/2 teaspoon of rosemary to the dry ingredients.

SWEDISH LIMPA BREAD

This is a cool-rising yeast bread.

One slice: 160 calories, 4 grams protein.

This recipe makes 2 loaves of 16 slices each.

1 package active dry yeast	1 tsp. salt
1/4 Cup warm water (105°-115°)	1/2 tsp. each: crushed caraway,
2 Cups cold milk	fennel, and anise seeds*
1/2 Cup molasses	Grated peel of 1 orange
1/2 Cup oil	(about 2 Tb.)
1/2 Cup rolled oats	1 Cup whole wheat flour
1/4 Cup packed brown sugar	6 to 7 Cups all-purpose flour

Dissolve yeast in warm water in a 7- or 8-quart bowl. Let stand 5 minutes. Add milk, molasses, oil, oats, sugar, salt, crushed seeds, and orange peel. Add whole wheat flour and mix well. Gradually add all-purpose flour, 2 cups at a time, stirring well after each addition so no flour pockets remain on the bottom or sides of bowl. Keep adding flour (about 6 or 7 cups) until dough looks and feels like it's just about ready to knead.

Cover dough securely with plastic wrap and let stand in a cool, draft-free place overnight or as long as 14 hours. Dough will rise to the top of the bowl. Sprinkle the top with 1/4 cup all-purpose flour and scrape down the sides of bowl. Turn out on a lightly floured table or countertop. Knead until smooth and elastic. Divide dough in half and shape each half into an oblong loaf. Place loaves in 2 9 x 5 x 3-inch loaf pans. Cover and let rise in a warm, draft-free place until doubled in size (about 1 hour).

Bake in 375° oven for 35 minutes or until loaves sound hollow when tapped. If the loaves brown too rapidly, cover the tops with foil.

---

*Crush seeds in a mortar with pestle or put inside a plastic bag and pound with a rolling pin or mallet.

POPOVERS

One popover: 137 calories, 6 grams protein.

This recipe makes 6 popovers.

2 eggs
3/4 Cup milk
1 Tb. oil
1 tsp. sugar
1/4 tsp. salt
1 Cup flour

Preheat oven to 450°. In a medium-sized bowl, beat eggs, milk, and oil together. Add sugar and salt. Slowly add flour and beat until the mixture is smooth and lump-free.

Spoon the batter into a well-greased, 6-cup muffin tin, filling each cup about 3/4 full. Bake at 450° for 15 minutes; then reduce heat to 350° and bake for another 15 to 20 minutes. Do *not* open oven while popovers are baking. These are best when served hot from the oven with strawberry jam or fresh sweet butter.

BLUEBERRY MUFFINS

One muffin: 160 calories, 4 grams protein.

This recipe makes 12 muffins.

2 Cups flour
3 tsp. baking powder
1/2 tsp. salt
1/3 Cup sugar
1 egg, slightly beaten
1 Cup milk
1/4 Cup vegetable oil
1 Cup fresh or frozen blueberries

Preheat oven to 375°. Mix 1 3/4 cups of the flour, baking powder, salt, and sugar in a large bowl. Add egg, milk, and oil, stirring only a few times—just enough to mix slightly. Batter should be lumpy. Sprinkle the remaining 1/4-cup flour over the blueberries. Gently fold berries into the batter. Spoon the batter into a greased or paper-lined 12-cup muffin tin. Fill each cup about 2/3 full. Bake at 375° for 20 minutes. Serve piping hot with a dollop of fresh sweet (unsalted) butter.

PEANUT BUTTER MUFFINS

One muffin: 206 calories, 8 grams protein.

This recipe makes 6 muffins.

1/3 Cup smooth or crunchy peanut butter
1/2 Cup milk
1 egg
1 Cup flour
3 Tb. sugar
2 tsp. baking powder
1/4 tsp. salt

Preheat oven to 350°. Mix peanut butter, milk, and egg together until smooth. Carefully fold in flour, sugar, baking powder, and salt. Do not overmix ingredients. Grease a 6-cup muffin tin or line tin with paper liners. Fill each cup 3/4-full with batter. Bake at 350° for 20 minutes.

CHEESE CORN BREAD

One square: 350 calories, 10 grams protein.

This recipe makes 9 squares.

1 package (8 1/2 oz.) corn bread mix
2 Tb. chopped onion
1 clove fresh garlic, chopped, or 1/4 tsp. garlic powder
1/2 tsp. oregano
1 egg
1/4 Cup vegetable oil
1/2 Cup milk
1/2 Cup creamed corn (canned)
1 1/2 Cups lightly packed shredded Cheddar cheese
OPTIONAL:
1 jalapeno pepper, fresh or canned, seeded, rinsed in cold water
    (to tone down flavor), and chopped
1 Tb. chopped black olives, for color
1 Tb. chopped pimiento, for color

Preheat oven to 375°. Mix together all the ingredients (including those that are optional), except 1/2 cup of the cheese. Pour batter into a lightly greased 9 x 9-inch cake pan. Sprinkle remaining cheese over corn bread. Bake at 375° for 30 minutes.

ZUCCHINI BREAD

One slice: 540 calories, 7 grams protein.

This recipe makes 1 loaf of 10 slices.

3 eggs
2 Cups sugar
1 Tb. vanilla
1 Cup oil
2 Cups all-purpose flour
2 tsp. cinnamon
1 tsp. nutmeg
2 tsp. baking soda
1/4 tsp. baking powder
1/2 tsp. salt
2 Cups grated zucchini, unpeeled
1 Cup chopped walnuts or 1/2 Cup raisins

Preheat oven to 350°. Beat eggs in a large mixing bowl. Gradually beat in sugar, vanilla, then oil. In a separate bowl combine the dry ingredients. Add to the egg mixture alternately with zucchini. Stir in walnuts or raisins. Turn into a greased loaf pan. Bake at 350° for 55 to 60 minutes or until bread tests done (a toothpick inserted into the center of the bread comes out clean).

EARLY AMERICAN SPOONBREAD

This is a simple dish to enjoy in the morning or as a light lunch—an old American favorite.

One serving: 230 calories, 9 grams protein.

This recipe serves 4.

2 Cups milk
1/2 Cup yellow cornmeal
2 Tb. margarine
2 eggs, beaten
1 tsp. salt

Preheat oven to 400°. Combine 1 cup of milk and the cornmeal in a heavy, medium-sized saucepan. Bring mixture to a boil over low heat. Gradually stir in the remaining cup of milk as the mixture begins to thicken. Add margarine. Continue stirring until the margarine melts completely and the mixture is smooth. Beat eggs and salt together and add to cornmeal mixture. Stir until well blended. Pour into a well-greased, 1-quart casserole or baking dish. Bake at 400° for 40 minutes or until the top turns a golden brown. Serve immediately. Top with brown sugar or fruit.

Soups with Substance

Soups, hot or cold, are the answer whenever a cancer patient is hungry, but can't think of a thing he'd like to eat. The soups that follow have enough character to encourage a faltering appetite. Some are almost as nutritious as a main dish: the Minestrone Soup, for example, provides 225 calories and 9 grams protein in one cup, and the Tomato Shrimp Bisque gives you 395 calories and 25 grams of protein in one cup.

If you're cooking for yourself, you'll find that blender soups are almost effortless because proportions and ingredients aren't rigid—you use whatever you have on hand.

If you're cooking for someone in the family who has cancer, you might find it worthwhile to double the amounts and freeze half. Since these soups are high-calorie and filling, they can also be the main item at family meals, followed by a light salad and dessert.

TOMATO-SHRIMP BISQUE

One cup soup: 395 calories, 25 grams protein.

This recipe makes slightly less than 3 cups.

1 can (10 oz.) condensed tomato soup
Equal amount (10 oz.) light cream or half & half
5 to 6 oz. small cooked shrimp
Thin lemon slices

Combine soup, cream, and shrimp in a medium-sized saucepan. Heat slowly to desired serving temperature. Do not boil. Serve with lemon slices. After serving, press soup spoon against the slices to add extra flavor to soup.

MUSHROOM BARLEY SOUP

A rich, hearty soup, to be accompanied by a thick slice of whole wheat bread.

One cup soup: 235 calories, 5 grams protein.

This recipe makes 6 cups.

1 Cup fresh mushrooms, sliced
2 Tb. onion, minced
1/2 green pepper, finely chopped
3 Tb. butter or margarine
2 Tb. flour
1/2 Cup beef bouillon
2 Cups milk
1 tsp. Worcestershire sauce
1/4 tsp. pepper
1/8 tsp. salt
1/2 Cup uncooked barley (quick-cooking variety)

Melt butter or margarine in a medium-sized saucepan. Saute' mushrooms, onion, and green pepper until soft. Sprinkle flour over vegetables and stir until vegetables are well coated. Continue cooking over medium heat until flour is browned. Gradually add bouillon and milk, alternately, and continue stirring. Add Worcestershire sauce, pepper, and salt. Stir in barley. Cover and simmer for about 15 minutes or until barley is tender.

NOTE: If soup becomes too thick after standing, simply add a little more milk.

MINESTRONE SOUP

A rich tomato-based soup—a meal in itself served with Cheese Corn Bread (page 82) or hot, buttered Popovers (page 79).

One cup soup: 225 calories, 9 grams protein.

This recipe makes 8 cups.

1/4 Cup olive oil
1 Cup chopped celery
1 large can (16 oz.) whole tomatoes, chopped, with juice, or 1 can (6 oz.)
    tomato paste and 2 Cups chicken consommé or bouillon
1 Cup chicken consommé or bouillon
1 bay leaf
1/2 tsp. oregano
1 tsp. basil
1/2 tsp. rosemary
1 clove fresh garlic, pressed
1 tsp. salt
1/2 tsp. pepper
2 Cups chopped vegetables, any combination—carrots, zucchini,
    green beans, peas, corn, potatoes
1 can (15 oz.) white navy beans or garbanzo beans (chick peas)
1 Cup uncooked spaghetti, broken, or 1 Cup uncooked elbow macaroni
1/2 Cup Parmesan cheese

Heat olive oil in a large soup kettle. Sauté celery until soft. Add tomatoes and 1 cup consommé or tomato paste and 3 cups consommé. Add seasonings and simmer for 10 minutes. Add chopped vegetable medley and simmer for 30 more minutes or until vegetables are soft. Add beans and pasta. Continue cooking until pasta is tender, about 7 to 10 minutes. Keep warm until ready to serve—soup should be very thick. Sprinkle each serving generously with Parmesan cheese.

QUICK VEGETABLE BLENDER SOUP

A simple soup base that really has no formal ingredients because it's made with whatever you have in your refrigerator. The recipe below tells you what procedures to follow.

One cup soup made with half & half: 135 calories, 7 grams protein.
One cup soup made with plain yogurt: 80 calories, 8 grams protein.

This recipe makes about 3 cups.

2 Tb. butter or margarine
1 medium onion, chopped
1 or 2 carrots, sliced
1 medium zucchini, sliced, or 1 handful of mushrooms, sliced, or
 1/2 seeded and diced medium cucumber
2 Cups or 1 can (15 oz.) chicken broth
1 Cup half & half or plain yogurt

Melt butter in a medium-sized skillet. Sauté vegetables until just about soft. Add chicken broth and gently simmer for about 5 minutes. Transfer to blender container. Add half & half or yogurt and purée. The version made with half & half is rich and creamy; the version made with yogurt is light and somewhat tart. Serve soup hot or chilled. Season liberally with parsley, fresh basil from your garden, salt and pepper.

CHILLED AVOCADO SOUP

One cup soup: 325 calories, 4 1/2 grams protein.

This recipe makes 2 cups.

1 can (8 oz.) V-8 juice
1/2 small onion, quartered
1 medium avocado, peeled, pitted, and thickly sliced
1/2 Cup sour cream
1 clove garlic, finely minced, or 1/4 tsp. garlic powder
1 tsp. fresh chopped basil or 1/2 tsp. dried basil
2 tsp. lemon juice
Salt and pepper to taste

Put all the ingredients into a blender and blend until a smooth liquid.
Chill. Garnish with chopped parsley.

CHILLED DILL SOUP

A cool, creamy summertime favorite.

One cup soup: 300 calories, 13 grams protein.

This recipe makes 4 cups.

1 1/2 Cups peeled and coarsely chopped cucumber (1 large cucumber)
1/2 Cup shelled walnuts
3 Tb. olive oil
1 Cup plain yogurt
1 Cup small curd cottage cheese
1 clove fresh garlic, pressed
2 tsp. fresh dill, or 1 tsp. dried dill, if fresh is not available
1 tsp. salt
1/4 tsp. pepper

Combine all ingredients in blender container. Blend on medium speed for 1 or 2 minutes. Serve immediately or refrigerate until ready to serve. Garnish with chopped dill or parsley.

CORN CHOWDER

One cup soup: 220 calories, 6 grams protein.

This recipe makes 6 cups.

2 Tb. butter or margarine
1 Cup chopped fresh onion
1/2 Cup chopped celery
1 1/2 Cups pared, diced potatoes
2 Cups fresh corn, cut from the cob, or 2 Cups drained, canned corn
1/2 tsp. salt
1/4 tsp. pepper
1 Cup chicken broth, canned or made with bouillon cube or concentrate
1/4 tsp. dried leaf thyme or summer savory
2 Cups whole milk
1 Cup half & half
OPTIONAL:
1/4 Cup bacon bits

Melt butter or margarine in a medium-sized saucepan. Add onion and celery and sauté until tender. Add potatoes, fresh corn, salt, pepper, chicken broth, and thyme or summer savory. Cover and simmer for 15 minutes or until potatoes are tender. If using canned corn, add for last 5 minutes. Add milk and half & half. Heat thoroughly, but don't allow to boil. Serve steaming hot, sprinkled with bacon bits if desired.

92

OLD COLONY PEANUT SOUP

One cup soup: 450 calories, 20 grams protein.

This recipe makes about 3 cups.

2 Tb. butter or margarine
1/4 Cup finely chopped onion
1/4 Cup finely chopped celery
1 Tb. flour
1 Cup chicken broth

1 1/2 Cups fortified milk*
1/2 Cup smooth peanut butter
Pinch of fresh grated nutmeg or
   a sprinkle of chili powder

Melt butter or margarine in a medium-sized skillet. Sauté onion and celery until soft. Sprinkle with flour, stirring constantly until smooth and thick. Slowly add chicken broth. Stir until mixture is thick and creamy. Add fortified milk and peanut butter. Continue stirring until smooth. Add nutmeg or chili powder. Stirring constantly, bring to a boil in order to fully thicken soup. Serve piping hot. Garnish with chopped peanuts or chopped parsley if you like.

Short on time? Try:

HURRY-UP PEANUT SOUP

One cup soup: 360 calories, 17 grams protein.

This recipe makes 4 cups.

1 can (10 1/2 oz.) cream of chicken soup
2 Cups fortified milk*

1/2 Cup smooth peanut butter
Pinch of nutmeg

Heat cream of chicken soup in medium-sized saucepan. Add fortified milk, peanut butter, and nutmeg and stir until well-blended and smooth.

---

*To make fortified milk, mix 1 quart whole milk with 1 cup powdered skim milk.

POTATO SOUP

One cup soup: 215 calories, 3 grams protein.

This recipe makes 6 cups.

3 Cups water or chicken broth (enough to cover vegetables)
3 medium potatoes, peeled and diced
1 medium onion, diced
1 Cup light cream or half & half
1/4 tsp. caraway seeds
2 Tb. dill weed or dried dill
1 tsp. salt
1/8 tsp. freshly ground pepper
1/2 Cup sour cream
2 Tb. butter

Bring water or broth to a boil in a large saucepan. Lower heat and add diced potatoes and onion. Simmer about 30 minutes or until vegetables are tender. Add cream, caraway seeds, dill, salt, and pepper. Simmer another 15 to 20 minutes or until soup begins to thicken and potatoes soften and separate a little. Mash potatoes lightly with potato masher if softening process needs helping along. Just before serving, stir in sour cream and butter. Allow to heat through, but not to boiling point. Serve immediately. Garnish with chopped chives, parsley, or dill if you wish.

GREEK LEMON SOUP

One cup soup: 225 calories, 10 grams protein.

This recipe makes 3 cups.

1 Cup chicken broth, homemade or canned
2 eggs
3 Tb. lemon juice
1/2 Cup heavy cream
1 Cup fresh-cooked rice
Salt and pepper to taste

Heat chicken broth to a near-boil in a 2-quart saucepan. Reduce heat to simmer.

In a small bowl, beat eggs until light in color. Stir in lemon juice and 3 tablespoons of hot chicken broth. Stir rapidly to prevent eggs from curdling.

Slowly add egg mixture to chicken broth in saucepan, stirring constantly until soup is smooth. Blend in cream, stirring rapidly. Stir in hot rice. Remove from heat. Salt and pepper to taste. Serve piping hot.

CONSOMMÉ WITH CREAM

One cup soup: 320 calories, 8 grams protein.

This recipe makes 3 cups.

1/4 medium onion
1/2 apple, cored and pared
2 Cups canned, condensed beef consommé
1 Cup heavy cream
1/4 tsp. salt
1/8 tsp. paprika
1/8 tsp. curry powder

Place onion and apple in blender container and chop by flicking on-off switch rapidly a few times. Add consommé and blend for 5 to 10 more seconds. Transfer mixture to medium-sized saucepan. Heat to simmer only. Slowly stir in cream. Add seasonings and serve with unsalted crackers.

Salads with Substance

When a cancer patient must force himself to eat, he can't afford to waste what little appetite he has on a salad of little nutritional value. Although crisp greens are often appealing, the time to eat them is when your appetite is up and you can supplement them with other dishes that provide calories and protein. Otherwise, try a salad with substance, like the salads in this section.

For example, one cup of Chicken Salad provides both 360 calories and almost one-half of a cancer patient's daily protein requirements. Just one-half cup of Lentil Salad provides 525 calories and 12 grams of protein.

If you're cooking for yourself, and feel tired, make a simple salad like the Stuffed Avocado or the Waldorf Salad. When you're feeling stronger, make the Tabbouli or the Lentil Salad and store for the next day.

If you're cooking for someone in the family who has cancer, notice that the salads that need cooking are in amounts sufficient for the main dish at a lunch or Sunday supper. Since these salads supply ample protein, your family will not be deprived of their protein needs.

CHICKEN SALAD

One cup: 360 calories, 44 grams protein.

This recipe makes 2 generous cups.

2 Cups cooked chicken,* diced
4 to 6 chilled water chestnuts, quartered**
Salt and pepper to taste
1 to 2 tsp. capers, drained
2 heaping Tb. mayonnaise
8 pecan halves, chopped
Few sprigs of parsley, snipped

Mix chicken, water chestnuts, salt, pepper, capers, and mayonnaise in order given. Sprinkle pecan bits and parsley over top of salad. Serve with hard-boiled egg slices dusted lightly with paprika. Particularly refreshing with a large glass of orange juice.

---

*See page 46 for poached chicken.

**An unopened can of water chestnuts can be stored in refrigerator for months. Once opened, transfer to a covered glass or plastic container—will keep ten days in refrigerator.

ALMOND CHICKEN MOUSSE

One-half cup: 289 calories, 18 grams protein.

This recipe makes 2 cups.

1 envelope unflavored gelatin
1/4 Cup cold water
1/4 Cup chicken broth
1 tsp. salt
1/2 tsp. pepper
1/2 tsp. thyme
1/2 Cup slivered almonds
2 egg yolks
2 Tb. lemon juice
1 Cup cooked chicken, diced
1/2 Cup heavy cream
Lettuce leaves or parsley for garnish

Soften gelatin in cold water for 5 minutes in a small saucepan. Dissolve over low heat. Place in blender container. Add chicken broth, salt, pepper, thyme, almonds, egg yolks, lemon juice, and cooked chicken. Blend until mixture is smooth, about 2 minutes, stopping to scrape down sides every 30 seconds. Whip cream. Fold blended ingredients carefully into whipped cream. Pour into a 9 x 5 x 3-inch loaf pan, and cover with foil. Chill in refrigerator until firm. Serve on cold platter, garnished with crisp greens or parsley.

TUNA SALAD

One-half cup: 215 calories, 18 grams protein.

This recipe makes 1 1/3 cups.

1 can (7 oz.) Albacore tuna,* well drained
1/2 Cup chopped celery or 1/2 Cup water chestnuts, quartered
2 Tb. lemon juice
1/4 Cup mayonnaise**
1 Tb. minced parsley
OPTIONAL (use one or more):
1 Tb. capers
1/4 Cup slivered almonds
1/2 medium apple, diced
2 hard-boiled eggs, chopped

Combine tuna, celery or water chestnuts, lemon juice, and mayonnaise in a medium-sized bowl. Toss until well mixed. Add parsley and any of the optional ingredients you choose. Serve chilled on a bed of lettuce or nestled between two slices of whole wheat bread.

---

*Albacore tuna (always identified on a can as fancy solid white tuna) is one of the two tuna species which is being netted without also killing dolphins. To protect dolphins, we encourage you to buy only this type of tuna.

**Try making your own mayonnaise (page 113). It takes only a few minutes and will give your tuna salad a fresh taste that no bottled mayonnaise ever could produce.

MACARONI WITH TUNA AND HERB SAUCE

When the salad is the supper for the entire family.

One cup: 235 calories, 17 grams protein.

This recipe makes about 10 cups.

3 Tb. olive oil
3 scallions, finely chopped (including green parts)
1 large clove garlic, finely chopped
1 tsp. dried marjoram or 2 tsp. fresh marjoram
Pinch dried thyme
1 Tb. lemon juice
1/2 Cup dry white wine
2 (7 oz.) cans Albacore tuna, drained
1/4 Cup fresh parsley, finely chopped
Freshly ground pepper to taste
1 lb. macaroni or pasta shells, uncooked

Heat oil in a small saucepan. Sauté scallions and garlic until scallions are just soft. Add marjoram and thyme. Continue cooking for a few minutes, then add wine and lemon juice and simmer gently for about 2 minutes. Remove from heat. Cook macaroni or shells according to package directions. Drain pasta and immediately toss in large bowl with flaked tuna and parsley. Pour sauce over mixture. Chill before serving.

STUFFED AVOCADO

Smooth and easy to eat.

One stuffed avocado half: 410 calories, 15 grams protein.

This recipe serves 2.

1 large ripe avocado
1 wedge fresh lemon
1 Cup cottage cheese
4 Tb. Thousand Island dressing

Cut avocado in half. Remove pit and discard. Squeeze lemon over each half to prevent avocado from blackening. Fill avocado halves with cottage cheese and top with dressing.

AVOCADO STUFFED WITH CRABMEAT OR SHRIMP

One stuffed avocado half: 360 calories, 8 grams protein.

This recipe serves 2.

1 large ripe avocado
1 wedge fresh lemon
1/2 Cup crabmeat or tiny cooked shrimp, fresh, canned, or
   frozen and defrosted
3 Tb. mayonnaise*
1/4 Cup chopped celery
1 Tb. fresh lemon juice
Paprika to taste

Open avocado as above. Squeeze lemon over avocado halves to prevent blackening. Pick any bits of cartilage from crabmeat; if using fresh shrimp, peel and devein before cooking. Mix with mayonnaise, celery, and lemon juice. Divide mixture in half and fill avocado halves, mounding slightly. Dust with paprika.

---

*For the freshest taste, make your own mayonnaise (page 113).

TABBOULI SALAD

This minty, fresh-tasting Lebanese salad offers an excellent source of protein.

One-half cup: 200 calories, 7 grams protein.

This recipe makes 4 cups.

1 Cup uncooked bulgar wheat*
2 Cups boiling water
2 Tb. lemon juice
1 can (15 oz.) chick peas (garbanzo beans)
2 Tb. olive oil
1 tomato, chopped
1/2 small onion, chopped
1/2 Cup fresh parsley, chopped
2 cloves fresh garlic, crushed
1/4 tsp. salt
1/4 tsp. pepper
2 tsp. chopped fresh mint or 1/4 tsp. crushed dried mint

Place bulgar wheat in a large mixing bowl. Pour water and lemon juice over wheat. Let stand for about 1 hour or until most of the water and juice has been absorbed. Add rest of ingredients and toss lightly to mix. Chill and serve on a bed of lettuce or fill pockets of toasted pita bread halves with Tabbouli and top with a spoonful of plain yogurt—makes a terrific sandwich.

---

*Bulgar wheat can be found in most health food stores or in the specialty or ethnic sections of some supermarkets. You'll find it well worth the trouble to track down this different and tasty grain.

LENTIL SALAD

A tangy salad loaded with protein.

One-half cup: 265 calories, 6 grams protein.

This recipe makes 4 cups.

1 Cup dry lentils
2 whole cloves garlic, peeled
3/4 Cup olive oil
1/2 tsp. salt
1/4 tsp. pepper
1 medium tomato, chopped
1/2 small onion, chopped
1/4 Cup vinegar

Wash lentils in colander, then transfer to a medium-sized saucepan. Add water to cover (2 to 3 cups) and garlic. Bring to a boil, then reduce heat to simmer. Simmer about 20 minutes or until lentils are tender. Be careful not to overcook—otherwise lentils will get mushy. Drain off water and discard garlic. Transfer lentils to a medium-sized bowl. Add rest of ingredients and toss to mix. Refrigerate until ready to serve.

COLD RICE SALAD

This is basically a "leftovers" salad—use the recipe as a guide, but don't be limited by it. Use whatever leftover vegetables and meats you have on hand.

One cup: 340 calories, 13 grams protein.

This recipe makes 4 cups.

1 Cup white rice, freshly cooked or leftover*
3 Tb. olive oil
2 to 3 Tb. wine vinegar
2 medium carrots, finely chopped
1 small onion, finely chopped
1 small green pepper, finely chopped
1 large rib celery, finely chopped
1/4 Cup fresh parsley, finely chopped
1 Cup cold diced beef, chicken, or ham
Salt and pepper to taste

Toss freshly cooked hot rice with oil and vinegar in a large salad or serving bowl. If you're using leftover rice, it should already be dressed.* Add remaining ingredients and toss well to mix. Salt and pepper to taste. Refrigerate until chilled and ready to serve.

---

*Leftover rice should be dressed with oil and vinegar (or lemon juice) before storing in refrigerator. Rice stored this way has more flavor and is ready to be tossed together into a salad at a moment's notice.

WALDORF SALAD

This recipe makes 4 cups.

3 firm, large, ripe apples, pared, cored, and quartered
2 Tb. lemon juice
1 Cup celery, chopped
1 Cup walnuts, coarsely chopped
1/2 Cup mayonnaise*

Slice quartered apples into small chunks. Toss with lemon juice in a medium-sized bowl (this keeps them from turning brown). Add celery and walnuts, then mayonnaise. Toss until apples are well coated. For an unusual combination of flavors, use two different kinds of apples— such as a tart green apple and a sweet red apple. Chill until ready to serve.

*See page 113 for mayonnaise recipe.

106

Sauces, Spreads, and Condiments

Sauces are a good way to boost the nutritional value of foods that are insufficient in calories and protein. Vegetables are a prime example of foods that need nutritional boosting. They are a good source of vitamins and minerals, but that's about all. Two tablespoons of Basic Cheese Sauce drizzled over one-half cup of broccoli will increase calories from 20 to 100. Two tablespoons of Basic White Sauce will increase the calories of one-half cup of iron-rich spinach from 18 to 70. Sauces also make swallowing easier because of the way they moisten foods.

Spreads serve both as an excellent source of calories and as boosters to the nutritional value of crackers and bread.

Condiments like the Pickled Lemon provide a mild and agreeable alternative to the spices some cancer patients can't tolerate.

If you're cooking for yourself, store sauce in a covered container in your refrigerator; it will keep for two or three days. When reheating, stir briskly with a whisk to dissolve any lumps that may have formed. Condiments store longer. For example, the Pickled Lemon can be kept for months in a covered jar on a shelf, and though it may darken, its flavor will not be affected.

If you're cooking for someone in the family who has cancer, remember that homemade mayonnaise and homemade sauces like hollandaise always taste fresher and lighter than the mass-produced bottled equivalents you find on supermarket shelves.

BASIC WHITE SAUCE

Two tablespoons of white sauce: 52 calories, 2 grams protein.

This recipe makes 1 cup.

2 Tb. butter
2 Tb. flour
1 Cup milk
1/2 tsp. salt
1/4 tsp. freshly ground pepper

Melt butter in a small, heavy saucepan. Add flour, stirring constantly with a wooden spoon until roux begins to bubble. Continue stirring about 2 more minutes—but be careful *not* to let the roux brown. Slowly add 1/2 cup of the milk, stirring constantly until sauce thickens. Gradually add remaining 1/2 cup of milk. Stir an additional 2 minutes. Remove from heat and add salt and pepper. If the sauce cools and thickens slightly, a skin may form. To remedy this, stir in a few drops of milk while reheating sauce. Stirring with a wire whisk can help smooth out any lumps that may form. This is a versatile sauce that can be used over fish, fresh vegetables, and eggs.

BASIC CHEESE SAUCE

Two tablespoons: 64 calories, 3 grams protein.

This recipe makes 1 1/4 cups.

Follow the procedure for Basic White Sauce, but add 1/2 cup grated Cheddar cheese during the last 2 minutes of cooking. Stir until smooth and creamy. Add a pinch of cayenne pepper if you like your sauce to have a bit of a "kick." Serve over fresh vegetables or fish or with a baked potato.

QUICK HOLLANDAISE SAUCE

Smooth, buttery, and tart.

Two tablespoons: 190 calories, 1 gram protein.

This recipe makes 1 1/4 cups.

2 egg yolks
1 1/2 Tb. boiling water
1 Cup (2 sticks) butter, melted
1 Tb. lemon juice
1/8 tsp. cayenne pepper
1/4 tsp. salt

Put egg yolks in blender container. Blend at low speed. Slowly add boiling water and then melted butter in a slow, thin stream. Add lemon juice and seasonings and continue to blend until sauce thickens. Taste—it may need more salt. Spoon over Baked Whitefish (page 126), Deviled Eggs (page 28), Salmon Loaf (page 129), or cooked broccoli or asparagus. A blanket of buttery hollandaise not only adds loads of calories, but also enhances the flavors of the foods above.

HERBED LEMON SAUCE FOR FISH

One-fourth cup: 250 calories, 4 grams protein.

This recipe makes about 1 1/2 cups—enough sauce for 4 servings of baked or broiled fish.

2 Tb. butter or margarine
2 Tb. flour
1/4 tsp. rosemary
1 Tb. chopped fresh parsley
1 1/2 Cups heavy cream
2 Tb. lemon juice
2 eggs, well beaten

Melt butter or margarine in small saucepan until foamy. Stir in flour, rosemary, and parsley. Blend well over low heat. Stir in cream and lemon juice (a wire whisk works especially well to keep sauce smooth and lump-free). Blend in eggs, stirring constantly for another 2 minutes. Serve over freshly baked or broiled fish.

SEAFOOD COCKTAIL SAUCE

One tablespoon: 12 calories.

This recipe makes 4 tablespoons.

3 Tb. ketchup
1 Tb. prepared horseradish
OPTIONAL:
2 to 3 drops Tabasco or other hot sauce
Juice from a slice of fresh lemon or lime

Mix ingredients together in a small bowl, adding optional ingredients if desired. Fresh lemon or lime juice will heighten the flavor of the basic ingredients. Serve with shrimp or crabmeat cocktail, oysters, or any firm-fleshed, cold, poached fish that can be flaked into a seafood cocktail.

REMOULADE SAUCE

Exquisite over cold cooked shrimp, crab, or lobster—allows delicate flavor of shellfish to emerge.

One tablespoon: 105 calories, 1 gram protein.

This recipe makes about 1 1/2 cups.

1 Cup mayonnaise
1 tsp. dry mustard
1 tsp. minced parsley
1 Tb. capers
1 hard-boiled egg, finely chopped
2 Tb. bottled chili sauce
1 clove fresh garlic, pressed
1 Tb. finely chopped anchovies or 1 tsp. anchovy paste

Blend mayonnaise with all other ingredients. Serve with cooked shellfish or over hard-boiled eggs or cooked asparagus spears. Store in covered container in refrigerator.

EASY BLENDER MAYONNAISE

Two tablespoons: 200 calories.

This recipe makes 1 cup.

1 egg
2 Tb. lemon juice or vinegar
1/2 tsp. salt
1/4 tsp. dry mustard
1 scant Cup vegetable oil

Place egg, lemon juice, salt, and mustard in blender container. Cover and process for a few seconds at low speed. Remove the small inset in the blender cover and, with motor still running at low speed, drizzle in oil through the opening in the cover. (Do not remove entire cover because contents will splash all over.) If your cover is in one piece, lift the corner and, with motor still running at low speed, drizzle in oil.

It's very important to add oil *slowly*, otherwise mayonnaise will not thicken properly. Stop blender if necessary to scrape down sides. Taste—add more lemon juice, vinegar, salt, or mustard, if needed. Refrigerate. Stays fresh about a week. Homemade mayonnaise adds a light, refreshing taste to salads and sandwiches—there's absolutely no substitute for it.

CHIVE MAYONNAISE

Follow procedure for Easy Blender Mayonnaise, but add 1/4 cup fresh chopped chives to mayonnaise. Delicious over baked or boiled potatoes, deviled eggs, or mixed with egg salad.

NOTE: To correct curdled mayonnaise (or hollandaise), whisk in a teaspoon or two of boiling water, a drop at a time. If that fails to work, place an egg yolk in a bowl and add the curdled sauce slowly, beating with a wire whisk. In time, you'll have a smooth, creamy sauce again—it takes only a little effort and a bit of patience to restore the sauce to its intended form.

HORSERADISH CREAM

A creamy, rather sharp accompaniment to slices of cold roast beef.

Two tablespoons: 60 calories.

This recipe makes 3/4 cup.

1/2 Cup sour cream
4 Tb. prepared horseradish
1 Tb. vinegar
1/4 tsp. salt

Stir ingredients together in a small bowl. Cover and refrigerate until needed—will keep about 2 weeks.

STRAWBERRY CREAM TOPPING

Two tablespoons: 110 calories, 2 grams protein.

This recipe makes about 1/2 cup.

2 Tb. sugar
1 package (3 oz.) cream cheese, softened to room temperature
1/2 Cup fresh or frozen strawberries (without syrup), coarsely chopped

Cream sugar and cream cheese together until soft and spreadable. Blend in strawberries and beat lightly until well mixed. Use a generous spoonful over Blender Waffles (page 34), Baked French Toast (page 33), Country Pound Cake (page 173), or Classic Sponge Cake (page 172).

BUTTER SPREADS FOR HOT FRENCH BREAD

Spreads can be stored covered in refrigerator.

One slice (2 1/2-inch) buttered French bread:
160 calories, 1 gram protein.

Each of the following recipes makes enough spread for 1 foot-long loaf of French bread.

HERB BUTTER

1/2 Cup butter or margarine,
  softened
1 clove garlic, minced, or
  1/4 tsp. garlic powder

1/4 tsp. basil
1/4 tsp. thyme
1/4 tsp. sweet marjoram

SESAME BUTTER

1/2 Cup butter or margarine,
  softened

2 Tb. cream cheese, softened
2 Tb. sesame seeds

BARBECUE BUTTER

1/2 Cup butter or margarine,
  softened
2 Tb. barbecue sauce

1 clove garlic, minced, or
  1/4 tsp. garlic powder

For each recipe: place all ingredients in a small mixing bowl and mix until well blended. Split loaf lengthwise. At 2 1/2-inch intervals, slice loaf almost to bottom. Butter generously with spread. Wrap in foil. Heat in warm (350°) oven for 5 to 7 minutes.

PICKLED LEMON

For those of you who no longer enjoy the taste of onion, here's a versatile substitute.

Quarter one lemon lengthwise almost to bottom. Pour a thin layer of salt in bottom of a sterile jar that will just contain lemon standing on end. Mash some salt into cut lemon and place in jar. Cover with tightly fitting lid. If using jar with metal cover, cover first with plastic wrap. Store for 2 weeks at room temperature. Turn jar upside down or shake from time to time. Salt will draw out more juice. After 2 weeks, lemon is ready to use and should be stored in refrigerator. Cut off tiny pieces as needed. Rinse before using to remove excess salt. Use to season lamb, any fish, tomatoes,* or in recipes calling for onion.

---

*Pickled lemon added to tasteless winter tomatoes magically gives them flavor. Use 1/4 slice pickled lemon finely chopped for 2 or 3 large, quartered tomatoes. For a tomato salad, add 2 tablespoons drained capers, 2 finely chopped ribs of celery with leaves, salt to taste, 1 or more hot fresh or canned rinsed peppers, and 1/4 cup olive or vegetable oil.

The Ten Most
Nutritious Vegetables

Few vegetables are high in calories, but they are good sources of vitamins and minerals. If you eat two of the following vegetables daily, you will fulfill your daily vitamin A and vitamin C requirements. To boost calories, serve vegetables with a small pat of butter or a sauce.

Acorn squash, 1/2, baked with 1 Tb. butter: 170 calories, 2 grams protein, 2,640 I.U.* vitamin A, 843 milligrams** potassium.

Broccoli, 1/2 cup, with 1 Tb. basic cheese sauce: 60 calories, 3 grams protein, 2,405 I.U. vitamin A, 52 milligrams vitamin C, 50 milligrams calcium, 196 milligrams potassium.

Carrots, 1/2 cup, cooked with 1 Tb. butter: 125 calories, 2 grams protein, 8,140 I.U. vitamin A, 172 milligrams potassium.

Collard greens, 1/2 cup, with 1 Tb. bacon drippings or butter: 120 calories, 2 grams protein, 5,780 I.U. vitamin A, 28 milligrams vitamin C, 150 milligrams calcium, 200 milligrams potassium.

Corn, 1/2 cup cooked with 1 Tb. butter: 170 calories, 3 grams protein, 290 I.U. vitamin A.

Lima beans, baby, 1/2 cup, with 1 Tb. butter: 205 calories, 6 grams protein, 355 milligrams potassium.

Peas, green, 1/2 cup, with 1 Tb. butter: 155 calories, 4 grams protein, 480 I.U. vitamin A, 108 milligrams potassium.

Potatoes, white, 1/2 cup au gratin: 175 calories, 6 grams protein, 375 milligrams potassium. 1/2 cup mashed, with 1 tsp. butter and 1 tsp. milk: 100 calories, 2 grams protein, 263 milligrams potassium.

Potatoes, sweet, candied, 1 piece 2 1/2" long, 2" diameter: 150 calories, 1 gram protein, 6,000 I.U. vitamin A, 180 milligrams potassium.

Spinach, 1/2 cup, with 1 Tb. basic white sauce: 60 calories, 3 grams protein, 8,100 I.U. vitamin A, 20 milligrams vitamin C, 342 milligrams potassium.

---

*An International Unit (I.U.) is a measure of the way a vitamin is utilized by the human body. It is not a measure of weight, like grams or milligrams.

**A milligram is 1/1000 of a gram.

Main Dishes to Serve Four

These recipes are main dishes in the conventional sense. They meet the requirements for high protein content and high calorie count so that one serving is all that a cancer patient needs to eat, even though the rest of the family might add a vegetable, bread, salad, and dessert. Many recipes, such as the Oriental Beef, the Baked Whitefish, the Hungarian Goulash, and the Mexican Chicken, provide almost one fourth of a cancer patient's daily protein needs.

If you're cooking for yourself, ask a friend to come over to help with the cooking and share the meal. Freeze any leftovers into one-person portions that can be reheated when you're not up to cooking.

If you're cooking for someone in the family who has cancer, these recipes offer first-class nutrition for the entire family. If you want to encourage a full meal for the person with cancer, suggest he work up an appetite by taking a walk before dinner—or by doing some simple exercises.

CHICKEN FRICASSEE

One serving: 300 calories, 24 grams protein.

This recipe serves 4.

2 to 3-lb. chicken, cut up into pieces
   or, if you prefer white meat,
   2 chicken breasts, split in halves
1 medium onion, quartered
1 carrot, sliced
3 Cups chicken broth, canned or
   made from bouillon cubes or
   concentrate
5 Tb. butter or margarine
5 Tb. flour
2 Tb. lemon juice
Salt and pepper to taste

OPTIONAL:
1 bay leaf
1/4 to 1/2 Cup small button
   mushrooms
3 Tb. butter or margarine
3 Tb. white wine

Simmer chicken with onion, carrot, and if desired, bay leaf, in chicken broth for about 30 minutes. When done, remove chicken and keep warm. Strain broth and reserve to use in sauce (carrot slices may also be reserved for later use).

Melt butter or margarine in a medium-sized saucepan. Add flour, stirring constantly until mixture begins to bubble. Gradually stir in chicken broth, and continue stirring until sauce thickens. Add lemon juice. Taste for seasoning. Add salt and freshly ground pepper as needed. Cut chicken meat in small pieces and add to sauce or add whole chicken pieces to sauce. (Carrot slices may also be added at this point.)

If desired, sauté mushrooms in butter or margarine. Add wine and simmer about 5 minutes or until liquid evaporates. Add to finished chicken fricassee.

Serve in pastry shells (Pepperidge Farm shells are especially nice) or over rice or Chinese noodles. Can be reheated. Garnish with fresh sprigs of parsley and mushrooms if you like.

BAKED CHICKEN PARMESAN

One serving (two pieces chicken): 335 calories, 25 grams protein.

This recipe serves 4.

2-lb. chicken, cut up into serving pieces
1/2 Cup bread crumbs
1/3 Cup Parmesan cheese
1 Tb. fresh parsley, chopped
4 Tb. margarine
1 Tb. Dijon mustard
1 clove garlic, finely minced, or 1/4 tsp. garlic powder

Preheat oven to 350°. In a medium-sized bowl, mix bread crumbs, cheese, and parsley together and set aside. Melt margarine in a medium-sized skillet. Add mustard and garlic. Dip each chicken piece into margarine mixture and then roll in the bread crumb, cheese, and parsley mixture. Place chicken pieces in a shallow roasting pan and pour remaining margarine mixture over chicken. Bake at 350° for 45 minutes to 1 hour, or until chicken tests done. Also delicious cold.

MEXICAN CHICKEN WITH RICE (ARROZ CON POLLO)

One serving: 480 calories, 30 grams protein.

This recipe serves 4.

2 1/2-lb. frying chicken, cut up into pieces
1/2 Cup vegetable oil
2 tsp. salt
1 tsp. pepper
2 tsp. oregano
1 clove fresh garlic, minced, or 1/2 tsp. garlic powder
1 medium green pepper, seeded and chopped
1/2 medium onion, chopped, or 1 jalapeno pepper, seeded,
   rinsed, and chopped
1 can (1 lb., 12 oz.) tomatoes (with juice), chopped
1 Cup rice, uncooked
1 Cup chicken broth or 1 chicken bouillon cube dissolved in 1 Cup boiling water
1 package (10 oz.) frozen peas
1/4 Cup green olives, chopped

Remove peas from freezer to thaw. Marinate chicken 10 to 15 minutes in salt, pepper, oregano, and garlic mixed with 6 tablespoons of the oil.

Heat remaining oil in a large skillet. Add chicken and brown about 10 minutes on each side. While chicken is browning, preheat oven to 350°.

Transfer chicken to 2-quart casserole. Add green pepper and onion or jalapeno pepper. Add chopped tomatoes with their juice, rice, and chicken broth. Mix gently.

Cover and bake at 350° for about 1 1/2 hours or until all liquid has been absorbed and rice is fluffy. Add thawed peas and olives, mixing in with a fork. Return to oven for an additional 5 minutes.

EASY CHICKEN CASSEROLE

This casserole is just as good the second day as it is the first.

One chicken breast: 460 calories, 28 grams protein.
One chicken leg: 350 calories, 18 grams protein.
One serving of noodles (one-half cup): 100 calories, 3 grams protein.

This recipe serves 4.

2 to 3-lb. frying chicken, cut up into pieces
3 Tb. vegetable oil
1 can (10 1/2 oz.) condensed cream of chicken soup
2 Cups sour cream
1/2 tsp. thyme
1/2 tsp. rosemary
1 large clove garlic, crushed, or 1 tsp. garlic powder
1 to 2 tsp. paprika, to taste
1/2 lb. green spinach or egg noodles

Heat oil in a large skillet. Brown chicken about 5 or 6 minutes on each side. Transfer chicken to a 2-quart casserole.

Preheat oven to 350°. Blend soup, sour cream, thyme, rosemary, and garlic together in a small bowl. Pour mixture over chicken in casserole. Cover and bake at 350° for 1 hour. Just before serving, sprinkle top liberally with paprika. Serve over bed of green spinach or egg noodles, cooked according to package directions. Refrigerate any leftovers in covered container.

MANDARIN STIR-FRIED CHICKEN

A flavorful source of high protein.

One serving: 360 calories, 36 grams protein.

This recipe serves 4.

3 Cups boned, uncooked chicken breasts (about 4), cut into small cubes
   with scissors or knife
3 Tb. sherry
1 Tb. soy sauce
1 Tb. cornstarch
1 1/4 tsp. freshly grated ginger root
2 Tb. sesame seeds
1/4 Cup peanut oil
10 small mushrooms
1/2 tsp. crushed red pepper
1 Cup snow peas
1 scallion, chopped

Marinate chicken cubes in mixture of two tablespoons sherry, the soy
sauce, the cornstarch, 1/4 teaspoon ginger, and the sesame seeds for
15 minutes. Heat peanut oil in a wok (or large skillet). Fry chicken for 2
minutes. Drain chicken and set aside. Pour off oil. Add remaining
sherry and ginger, mushrooms, and red pepper and stir for 2 minutes.
Add snow peas and scallion and stir 1 minute before adding chicken.
Stir until chicken is well coated with sauce. Serve over fried Chinese
noodles or rice. One-half cup Chinese noodles provides 110 calories, 3
grams protein; one-half cup rice provides 110 calories, 2 grams protein.

TURKEY OR CHICKEN HASH

One serving: 340 calories, 25 grams protein.

This recipe serves 4.

4 Tb. butter
4 Tb. flour
1 1/2 Cups chicken stock or chicken broth
2 Cups cooked turkey or chicken, cubed
1/4 Cup heavy cream*
2 egg yolks
1 Tb. sherry or dry white wine
Salt and pepper to taste

Melt butter in a medium-sized skillet. Make a roux by stirring in flour. Stir continuously with wooden spoon until mixture begins to bubble. Slowly add chicken stock, stirring constantly to avoid lumping, and simmer 4 to 5 minutes. Add turkey or chicken cubes. Combine cream and egg yolks in small bowl. Fold into hash in skillet. Add sherry or wine, salt and pepper to taste. Serve over toast or in pastry shells.

*Leftover heavy cream (unwhipped whipping cream) freezes well in its own carton.

BAKED WHITEFISH

Delicious, easy to prepare—and since it's baked wrapped in foil, it doesn't smell while cooking.

One serving: 450 calories, 42 grams protein.

This recipe serves 4.

3-lb. whitefish (or any other firm-fleshed fish), boned, cleaned,
   and with head removed*
1/2 lemon, sliced
1/2 tsp. salt
1/2 tsp. pepper
4 Tb. butter, thinly sliced
1/2 medium onion, thinly sliced
2 tsp. parsley
1 Tb. paprika

Preheat oven to 350°. Wash and dry fish. Rub with lemon slices—this keeps fish flesh white and firm. Place fish, open, on two large sheets of heavy aluminum foil, oiled so that fish won't stick. Sprinkle fish with salt and pepper. Place about three-quarters of the butter slices on one-half of the fish. Top with onion slices and a sprinkle of parsley. Fold over other half of fish and place remaining butter slices on top. Wrap tightly in foil. Place on baking sheet or in shallow pan and bake at 350° for 45 to 50 minutes. When done, remove foil, transfer to serving dish, and sprinkle with paprika. Decorate with lemon wedges and parsley. Serve with Herbed Lemon Sauce for Fish (page 110), if you like. Serve leftovers cold with mayonnaise.

---

*If you can do so, always buy fresh fish, rather than frozen, as frozen fish loses some texture and flavor. If you must use frozen fish, thaw it in milk—you will find that this helps to restore its flavor.

BASIC BROILED FISH

One serving: 475 calories, 43 grams protein.

This recipe serves 4.

2 lb. fresh or frozen (thawed) whitefish fillet or lake trout
6 Tb. butter
2 Tb. flour
1 Tb. paprika
3 Tb. butter, melted
1 tsp. Worcestershire sauce or soy sauce
1 Tb. lemon juice

Place fish on oiled foil in shallow baking pan, skin side down (if any skin). Top with little dots of butter, a light dusting of flour (sprinkle from your hand or through a sieve), and paprika. The flour keeps the fish from leaking its juices and makes a light crust. Grill under broiler for 5 to 7 minutes on each side, until fish flakes easily when tested with fork. Before serving, pour mixture of the melted butter, Worcestershire (or soy) sauce, and lemon juice over fish.

FISH VERACRUZ

The Veracruz sauce is a wonderful disguise for ordinary frozen fish fillets. On fresh snapper, it creates a splendid dish.

One serving: 450 calories, 42 grams protein.

This recipe serves 4.

SAUCE:

1/3 Cup olive or vegetable oil	12 pitted green olives, cut
1 clove garlic, minced	into rings
1 medium onion, minced	4 medium tomatoes, chopped, or
2 pimientos, drained and chopped	one 16-oz. can tomatoes,
1 Tb. each: capers, chili powder,	chopped
and lemon juice	1/4 Cup water
1 tsp. salt	
1/4 tsp. each: pepper, cinnamon,	
cloves, and nutmeg	

FISH:

1 1/2 lb. fresh or frozen (thawed) red	3 Tb. butter
snapper, bass, channel catfish,	2 Tb. flour
cod, or haddock	3 or 4 apple slices

SAUCE: Heat olive or vegetable oil in a medium-sized saucepan. Add garlic and onion and sauté until transparent. Add rest of sauce ingredients in order given. Simmer 10 minutes.

FISH: While sauce simmers, rinse fish fillets in a bowl of cool water, drain, and pat dry with paper towels. Dust fish with flour and shake off any excess. Melt butter in a large skillet. Sauté fish lightly with a few apple slices to reduce odor of sautéing. Transfer fish to baking dish. Preheat oven to 375°. Pour sauce over fish and bake at 375° for 30 minutes. Arrange fish on a platter surrounded by thin slices of French bread fried in butter and serve.

SALMON LOAF

An excellent source of protein that's easy to prepare.

One serving: 330 calories, 28 grams protein.

This recipe serves 4.

1 egg
1/2 Cup milk
1 Cup soft bread crumbs
1 can (1 lb.) salmon
1 tsp. lemon juice
1/2 tsp. salt
1/4 tsp. pepper
1 tsp. sweet basil
1/4 Cup chopped parsley

Preheat oven to 350°. Beat egg and milk together in a medium-sized bowl. Add bread crumbs. Flake salmon and remove any bones or skin. Add to egg mixture along with the remaining ingredients and mix thoroughly. Transfer to a lightly greased 8 1/2 x 4 1/2 x 2 1/2-inch loaf pan. Bake at 350° for about 30 minutes. Serve plain or with Basic White Sauce (page 108). Leftovers are good cold with mayonnaise.

HUNGARIAN GOULASH

One serving Hungarian Goulash: 520 calories, 29 grams protein.
One cup noodles: 200 calories, 6 grams protein.

This recipe serves 6.

3 Tb. butter or vegetable oil
1/2 medium onion, chopped
3 Tb. sweet Hungarian paprika
1 lb. lean beef, cubed (1 1/2-inch cubes)
1 lb. lean pork, cubed (1 1/2-inch cubes)
2 Tb. flour
1 tsp. salt
1/2 tsp. pepper
2 (10 1/2 oz.) cans beef broth or 3 Cups bouillon or beef stock
1 bay leaf
3 oz. (1/2 6 oz. can) tomato paste
1 Cup sour cream

Melt butter or heat oil in a large skillet. Add onion and sauté until soft. Stir in paprika and simmer slowly for 1 to 2 minutes. Roll meat in flour and add to skillet. Brown lightly. Sprinkle with salt and pepper. Add broth, bay leaf, and tomato paste. Cover and simmer over low heat about 1 hour or until meat is tender. Add sour cream and heat gently. Do not boil. Can be reheated. Serve over a bed of buttered egg noodles.

ORIENTAL BEEF

One serving Oriental Beef: 290 calories, 35 grams protein.
One cup rice: 160 calories, 3 grams protein.

This recipe serves 4.

1 flank or round steak, 1 1/2 to 2 lb.
2 Tb. vegetable oil or sesame oil*
1 clove garlic, minced
2 tsp. soy sauce
1/8 tsp. fresh ginger root, grated, or 1/4 tsp. ground powdered ginger
2 medium green peppers, seeded and cut into strips
2 fresh tomatoes, quartered
1 Tb. cornstarch
1/4 Cup water

Cut beef into paper-thin slices about 2-inches long. Heat oil in a medium-sized skillet. Add beef and brown. Add garlic and cook 2 to 3 minutes. Add soy sauce and ginger. Cover and reduce heat. Simmer slowly for 5 minutes. Mix in peppers and tomatoes. Make a paste of cornstarch and water. Add to pan, stir until sauce thickens, about 3 minutes. Serve over fluffy white rice.

---

*Use sesame oil to add that authentic Chinese flavor. It can be found in Chinese food markets and some health food stores.

HAMBURGERS ADAPTED FROM JULIA CHILD

One serving: 500 calories, 25 grams protein.

This recipe serves 4.

1 lb. lean ground beef, the leaner the better
5 1/2 Tb. butter, softened
1 Cup fresh sliced mushrooms
1 tsp. salt
1/8 tsp. pepper
1/8 tsp. summer savory
1 egg
SAUCE:
1/4 Cup beef bouillon
1/2 Cup heavy cream
Salt and pepper to taste
Sprinkle of nutmeg
2 Tb. butter
2 Tb. minced parsley or chives or both

Mix beef, 1 1/2 tablespoons of the softened butter, seasonings, and egg until nicely blended. Wet your hands and shape mixture into 4 patties (wet hands make handling easier). Melt remaining 4 tablespoons of butter in a large skillet and allow it to foam. Reduce heat and sauté mushrooms. When mushrooms are about half-sautéed, move to sides of pan and add hamburgers. Cook 6 to 12 minutes, depending upon how well-done you like your meat. Turn frequently (once each minute) to keep them juicy. Remove with mushrooms to heated platter. Cover and keep warm.

SAUCE: To the same skillet add 1/4 cup canned bouillon. Boil down rapidly while stirring any leftover cooking juices into bouillon. Add heavy cream and continue stirring to thicken slightly. Add salt, pepper, and nutmeg. Reduce heat and add butter and parsley or chives. Spoon over hamburgers. Serve immediately.

OVEN BAKED PORK CHOPS WITH APPLES

One serving: 365 calories, 20 grams protein.

This recipe serves 4.

4 pork chops, about 1 1/2 inches thick
2 Tb. flour
Salt to taste
Freshly ground pepper to taste
2 Tb. vegetable oil
3 apples, peeled, cored, and sliced
1/2 Cup chicken stock or apple juice
A pinch of crumbled thyme or rosemary leaves, or both

Lightly dust the pork chops with flour and shake off any excess.
Sprinkle with salt and pepper. Heat oil in Dutch oven and brown pork
chops over medium heat, covered, for 5 minutes on each side. Meanwhile, preheat oven to 350°. Add apples, liquid, and thyme or rosemary
to pan. Cover again and bake in a 350° oven for 50 minutes. Especially
nice with mashed potatoes or noodles.

SWEET AND SOUR PORK

One serving: 485 calories, 20 grams protein.

This recipe serves 4.

1 lb. pork tenderloin, cut into
  1-inch cubes
1 tsp. sesame oil, or
  vegetable oil
2 Tb. sherry
3 Tb. honey
1 tsp. fresh ginger root, grated, or
  1 tsp. powdered ground ginger
2 Tb. cornstarch
1 egg white

1/4 Cup vinegar
1/2 Cup water
2 tsp. soy sauce
1 tsp. cornstarch mixed with
  2 Tb. water
3 Tb. vegetable oil
2 small green peppers, seeded and
  cut into 1-inch cubes
1/2 Cup fresh or canned pineapple, cut into 1-inch chunks

The key to fast, easy Chinese cooking is in the preparation—have all your ingredients ready (cut and grated) *before* you start cooking. Parboil* pork in 1-quart saucepan for 5 minutes. Remove with slotted spoon to small bowl. Marinate pork cubes in mixture of sesame oil or vegetable oil, sherry, 1 tablespoon honey, and ginger for half an hour. Mix cornstarch with egg white to make a paste and add to marinated pork, mixing until all pork cubes are coated. In a small bowl combine remaining two tablespoons honey, vinegar, water, soy sauce, and cornstarch/water mixture and set aside. Heat oil in a large skillet. Fry pork cubes for 5 minutes, browning all sides. Drain pork on paper towel. Remove oil from skillet and return skillet to heat. Add vinegar mixture and stir until sauce begins to thicken. Add green peppers and continue stirring until sauce is very thick and peppers are slightly cooked. Add pineapple chunks and pork cubes and stir gently until well coated with sauce and heated through. Serve over fried Chinese noodles or rice. One-half cup Chinese noodles provides 110 calories, 3 grams protein, and one-half cup rice gives you 80 calories, 2 grams protein.

---

*To parboil means to partially cook a food by quick immersion in just enough boiling water to cover.

VEAL SCALLOPINE

Veal scallops (cutlets) in Marsala wine sauce are a delicacy loved the world over—and are surprisingly easy to prepare.

One serving: 305 calories, 22 grams protein.

This recipe serves 4.

1 lb. veal cutlets (cut from the leg),* pounded thin
Salt and freshly ground black pepper to taste
3 Tb. flour
3 Tb. margarine
1/2 Cup dry Marsala wine
Finely chopped parsley for garnish

Season veal cutlets lightly with salt and pepper. Dust with flour and shake off any excess. Heat margarine in a 10- or 12-inch skillet until it melts and bubbles. Sauté cutlets about 1 minute on each side over medium heat. Do not crowd pan. As cutlets are done, remove to heated platter or warm oven. Add Marsala wine to skillet and cook over high heat until reduced by half. Return veal cutlets to skillet, baste in sauce. Arrange cutlets on platter, top with remaining sauce from skillet, and serve immediately. Sprinkle with parsley if desired.

---
*Although veal has a delicate flavor all its own, you may also prepare this recipe substituting slices of boned, pounded chicken or turkey breast. Ask your butcher to pound the meat for you.

BAKED GREEN NOODLES

One serving: 470 calories, 27 grams protein.

This recipe serves 6.

1 1/2 lb. lean ground beef
1 large clove garlic, crushed, or 1/2 tsp. garlic powder
2 (8 oz.) cans tomato sauce
1 (8 oz.) can tomato paste
1/2 tsp. basil, use fresh if possible
1/4 tsp. oregano
1/4 tsp. salt
1/8 tsp. freshly ground pepper
1 Cup sliced mushrooms, fresh or canned
1/2 Cup sour cream
1/2 lb. green spinach noodles
1/4 to 1/2 Cup grated Parmesan cheese

Cook noodles according to package directions. While noodles are cooking, brown meat in a heavy, medium-sized skillet. Add garlic to meat and continue cooking for an additional 5 minutes. Add tomato sauce, tomato paste, seasonings, mushrooms and sour cream. Blend well. Preheat oven to 350°.

Spread half the noodles over bottom of a buttered 2-quart casserole. Ladle enough meat sauce over noodles to cover them. Spread remaining noodles over this. Top with remaining meat sauce. Cover casserole. Bake, covered, at 350° for 25 to 30 minutes. Remove from oven. Sprinkle liberally with grated Parmesan cheese. Return to oven, uncovered. Bake an additional 5 minutes, until cheese is golden brown and forms a crust.

SIMPLE SPAGHETTI CARBONARA

A modern Roman favorite.

One serving: 621 calories, 32 grams protein.

This recipe serves 4.

4 slices bacon, cut in narrow strips about 1 1/2-inches long
3 thin slices packaged ham, cut in narrow strips, (3 oz.)
1 lb. spaghetti, uncooked
3 eggs, beaten
1 Cup grated Parmesan cheese
Freshly ground black pepper to taste

Fry bacon strips in small skillet. When brown, add ham and keep warm. Start cooking spaghetti at this point, following package directions. In the meantime, beat eggs with Parmesan cheese in a medium-sized bowl. When spaghetti is cooked, drain and transfer to large, *warm* bowl. Immediately add bacon, ham, and egg/cheese mixture. The heat of the spaghetti cooks the egg—the end result should be a creamy sauce coating the pasta. Sprinkle with freshly ground pepper to taste and more grated Parmesan.

FETTUCCINE ALFREDO

One serving: 690 calories, 14 grams protein.

This recipe serves 4.

1/2 lb. fettuccine or thin noodles
1/4 lb. (1 stick) butter or margarine, melted
1 Cup heavy cream, warmed
1/2 Cup grated Parmesan cheese
1/2 tsp. salt
1/4 tsp. freshly ground pepper

Warm a large, oven-proof bowl or casserole dish in the oven. Cook noodles according to package directions and drain. Transfer noodles to warm bowl and quickly add remaining ingredients. Toss briefly to coat noodles. Serve immediately.

A Note Concerning Meat Recipes

Because many cancer patients do not like the taste of meat while they are in treatment, we have included only a limited number of meat recipes here. For those who do like meat, the following table shows the amount of protein and number of calories provided by one three-ounce serving, unless otherwise indicated, of a variety of meats. Also included are the protein content and calorie count for three-ounce portions of fish and fowl.

	Grams Protein	Calories
Beef		
Plain grilled hamburger patty	20	240
Roast beef	20	300
Steak/sirloin	20	300
Pot roast (chuck roast)	21	280
Corned beef	21	315
Calves' liver, fried	25	220
Pork		
Pork roast	21	300
Pork chops	20	230
Ham/Bacon		
Ham, 1 slice	15	210
Broiled bacon, 3 slices	6	150
Lamb		
Lamb roast	21	235
Lamb chops	20	260
Veal		
Breast of veal	21	255
Chicken		
Baked chicken, 1/2 breast	25	115
Chicken livers, sautéed	20	120
Fried chicken, 1/2 breast	25	160

	Grams Protein	Calories
Fish		
Fish sticks (frozen)	12	150
Cod or haddock fillets	14	140
Herring in cream sauce	15	150
Salmon, canned	22	180
Albacore tuna		
in oil	27	165
in water	27	125
Turkey		
Roasted (light or dark meat)	27	160
Sausage		
Summer sausage, 1 slice (1 ounce)	5	85
Frankfurters, 1	5	110
Bologna, 1 slice (1 ounce)	3	85
Liver sausage (1 ounce)	4	90
Salami, 1 slice (1 ounce)	4	75

Cooking with Herbs

The herbs you grow yourself have a special freshness and delicacy of flavor. Even when you dry them (or freeze them) at summer's end, they have more flavor than those you buy in supermarkets.

Herbs are easy to grow. Some, such as basil, chervil, dill, parsley, and summer savory, grow from seed, while most others are better bought as plants or grown from cuttings.

Don't worry too much about which herbs go with what. Experiment a little. Most green herbs can be snipped and mixed together and sprinkled on fish, salads, or cottage cheese. (A few exceptions: bay, rosemary, and thyme have stiff leaves and sage is probably too strong in flavor. Use these in casseroles or on roasts.)

In cooking, use twice the quantity of fresh herbs as you would use with dried herbs. Add fresh herbs near the end of cooking; they release their flavor quickly.

Herewith, some notes on a few of the most popular and useful herbs, followed by a list of seed and plant sources:

BASIL *(Ocimum basilicum):* annual, grows from seed, likes sun. A sweet, spicy herb, wonderful with tomatoes, Mediterranean dishes, almost anything else. Bush basil (if you can find plants) can be propagated in water from cuttings. Bush basil has small leaves, a sweeter, lighter flavor than garden basil, and is the favored basil of Italy, especially for *pesto* (recipe included in this book).

BAY *(Laurus nobilis):* perennial. Likes shade. Buy a plant if you can find it. Marvelous in soups and stews.

CELERY: leaves can be used fresh or dried (dry in warm oven). Store in covered jar. Good in salads, soups, stews, poultry stuffing.

CHERVIL *(Anthriscus cerefolium):* annual, grows from seed, needs shade. Winter indoors. A spicy parsley flavor, delicate ferny leaves. One of the classic French *fines herbes.* Good in soup, stews, or snipped fresh on many dishes.

CHIVES *(Allium schoenoprasum):* perennial. Likes sun. To winter inside, cut back after frost, dig up, and bring indoors. With potted chives from the store, cut back and put in refrigerator for a couple of weeks to let go dormant; plant will come back in abundance instead of going spindly and brown. Chive blossoms (blue flowers) have an onion taste similar to that of chive leaves; they are good sprinkled on scrambled eggs or on salad.

GARLIC CHIVES *(Allium tuberosum):* has straplike leaves, with garlic flavor. Also perennial, likes sun.

DILL *(Anethum graveolens):* annual, needs full sun, grows from seed. Finely chopped fronds are good with potatoes, vegetables, salad, fish.

MARJORAM *(Origanum majorana):* tender perennial, likes sun. Can be grown from seed. Goes into almost everything.

MINT: *(Mentha spicata or viridis)* spearmint; *(M. rotondifolia)* applemint; *(M. piperita)* peppermint. Perennials, like shade, grow from cuttings. Use fresh or dried. Good on fruit, in salad, on meat, even on fish, chopped with other herbs. A sprig of fresh mint enhances iced tea.

OREGANO *(Origanum vulgare):* hardy perennial, likes sun, can be grown from seed. Stronger flavor than sweet marjoram, which it closely resembles. Good in Greek and other Mediterranean dishes. Imported dried Greek oregano has the best flavor because of soil it grew in.

PARSLEY *(Petroselinum crispum)*—curly parsley; *(P. neopolitanum)* —Italian flat-leaved parsley: both are biennials, taste best their first year. Like sun, can be grown from seed but take up to 6 weeks to germinate. Flat-leaf parsley has fuller flavor. Both kinds have a clean, fresh taste and will take odor of raw onions off the breath.

ROSEMARY *(Rosmarinus officinalis):* a woody evergreen with a wonderfully aromatic piney fragrance and tiny blue blossoms. Winter indoors. Grows best from cuttings. Use leaves, fresh or dried. Good with pork and chicken.

SAGE *(Salvia officinalis):* a shrubby perennial. Likes sun. Best grown from cuttings. Use fresh or dried. Good in poultry stuffing and pork.

SAVORY *(Satureia hortensis):* annual. Likes sun. Summer savory—sweeter and less pungent than winter savory *(S. montana),* which is perennial. A mild, all-purpose herb that freshens stews, soups, roasts (also tones down the strong flavor of such vegetables as cabbage and Brussels sprouts). Makes old green beans taste young and fresh.

TARRAGON *(Artemisia dracunculus):* perennial. Likes sun. Does *not* grow from seed (skip Russian tarragon, which does grow from seed but tastes like crabgrass). Use fresh or dried in salads and in chicken and egg dishes.

Write to any of the following for fresh herb plants. Order from the closest source so that the herbs stay in their own climate. Bush basil, chives, garlic chives, parsley, rosemary, chervil, bay, and mint will grow indoors on a windowsill. All other herbs want sunny outdoor space. If you're not interested in herb gardening, buy dried herbs in leaf form and crumble them as you use them. They'll always reward you with better flavor than powdered herbs.

Sunnybrook Farms Nursery (plants only)
P.O. Box 6
9448 Mayfield Road
Chesterland, Ohio 44026

Casa Yerba, Rare Herb Seeds and Plants
Star Route 2, Box 21
Days Creek, Oregon 97429

Well Sweep Herb Farm
Mt. Bethel Road
Port Murray, New Jersey 07865

Taylor's Herb Gardens
1535 Lone Oak Road
Vista, California 92083

Otto Richter & Sons, Ltd.
Box 26A
Goodwood, Ontario L0C 1A0
Canada (seeds only for export)

Growing Herbs in Pots, by John Burton Brimer (Fireside, 1978), paperback, may be useful if you do decide to grow your own.

Clay Pot Cooking/
Crock Pot Cooking

Clay Pot Cooking

Clay pot cooking began when the cavemen discovered that freshly killed game wrapped in wet clay and baked over hot coals stayed moist and tender.

Cooking in an unglazed clay pot isn't very different. Put poultry or meat or fish in the pot, with vegetables, herbs, and seasoning for extra flavor, then cover tightly to keep moisture and flavor in.

Food cooked in clay pots does not need tending once in the oven—meat bastes itself with its own juices. And there's no cooking smell, because the clay pot holds in the aromas.

Clay pots come with basic cooking instructions and, if you like to improvise, these instructions are all you need.

Crock Pot Cooking

Crock pot cooking is the way to come home to a hot meal after you've been out most of the day. Put the ingredients in the crock pot in the morning and start the pot, for long, slow cooking. Slow cooking tenderizes cheaper cuts of meat and adds extra flavor, since the meat stews in its own juices. Most crock pots come with their own recipe books and emphasize meats.

Liquid and Cool

These nonalcoholic drinks are a nice change from the monotony of juices that sometimes offset nausea. They are also a welcome relief when solid food is unpalatable. The recipes that follow provide good calorie counts and the crushes even contribute decent protein. The drinks made with the ice are especially soothing if your mouth or throat are sore.

If liquids are the easiest form of nourishment at this time, increase the calorie count of any drink by adding Polycose, (see page 195).

If you're cooking for yourself and need a blender, check with your local chapter of the American Cancer Society. It may just have one to lend you.

If you're cooking for someone in the family who has cancer, re member that these drinks will taste best when freshly made. Many of them can be made without a blender. Use a jar with a screw top. Crush needed ice cubes in a plastic bag (use a rolling pin or the flat side of a hammer) and transfer ice to the jar. Add ingredients, cover jar, and shake vigorously.

COCONUT FLIP

One cup: 195 calories, 4 grams protein.

This recipe serves 2.

1/2 Cup shredded coconut
1 Cup milk
3 Tb. fresh lemon or lime juice
4 ice cubes

Combine coconut, milk, and lemon or lime juice in blender container. Blend for 1 minute. Add ice cubes and blend another minute or until ice is completely crushed. Or, use jar-and-crushed-ice technique.

LEMONADE (OR LIMEADE)

Refreshing and cool—a real thirst-quencher on a hot summer day.

One glass: 45 calories.

This recipe serves 1.

1 glass (8 oz.) water
Juice of 1 fresh lemon or lime or 2 Tb. bottled lemon or lime juice
1 or 2 tsp. honey or sugar to taste*
Fresh mint

Combine water, juice, and sweetener in blender container. Blend for a few seconds. If you add ice to blender, you can make a refreshing lemonade or limeade slush. Of, if you prefer, simply pour blended juice over ice cubes in a tall, chilled glass. Serve with fresh mint.

---

*Lime juice may need more sweetener.

LEMON SLUSH

One glass: 139 calories, 3 grams protein.

This recipe serves 1.

1 egg white*
5 or 6 ice cubes
3 Tb. lemonade drink mix powder

Put egg white and ice together in blender and blend. Add dry ingredients and blend until drink is a thick slush. Or, use jar-and-crushed-ice technique.

*Since egg white is to be used raw, make sure the eggshell isn't cracked or broken. If in doubt, use egg only in cooked dishes.

FRESH ORANGE CRUSH

One cup: 140 calories, 7 grams protein.

This recipe serves 1.

1 navel orange, peeled and sectioned
1 egg*
2 Tb. lemon juice
1 or 2 ice cubes

Combine all ingredients in blender container. Blend for 20 to 30 seconds.

*Since egg is to be used raw, make sure the eggshell isn't cracked or broken.

ORANGE-BANANA JUICE

One glass: 194 calories.

This recipe serves 1.

1 Cup orange juice
1 ripe banana

Put all ingredients in blender container and blend at medium speed until smooth. Serve in tall glass over ice.

BANANA-YOGURT SHAKE

One tall glass: 235 calories, 14 grams protein.

This recipe serves 1.

1/2 Cup whole milk
1/2 Cup plain yogurt
1 ripe banana

Pour milk into blender container. Add yogurt and banana. Blend until smooth, about 30 seconds. Serve in a tall glass.

NOTE: Any other fruit can be used with or in place of the banana. For example, ripe strawberries, fresh or canned peaches, or blueberries.

To increase calories:
Two teaspoons of honey added to the shake will increase calories to 276 per glass.

APRICOT (OR PEACH) FLIP

One cup: 164 calories.

This recipe serves 1.

1/2 Cup canned, drained apricots or peaches
1/4 Cup orange juice
1 or 2 ice cubes

Combine all ingredients in blender container. Blend for 30 seconds or until smooth. Serve in a tall, chilled glass.

PEACH EGGNOG

One cup: 236 calories, 11 grams protein.

This recipe serves 1.

1/2 Cup milk
5 peach slices, fresh or canned
1 egg*

Combine milk and peaches in blender container. Blend about 15 seconds. Add egg and blend another 10 seconds. Serve in tall glass.

---

*Since egg is to be used raw, make sure the eggshell isn't cracked or broken.

153

PINEAPPLE SMOOTHIE

One cup: 230 calories, 9 grams protein.

This recipe serves 1.

1/4 Cup crushed pineapple, with juice
1/2 Cup vanilla yogurt
1/2 Cup milk
1 tsp. lemon juice

Combine all ingredients in blender container. Blend for 20 to 30 seconds, until smooth. Or, vigorously shake ingredients together in a covered jar. Serve in a tall glass.

PEANUT BUTTER SHAKE

One cup: 303 calories, 12 grams protein.

This recipe serves 1.

1/2 Cup cold milk
2 Tb. nonfat powdered milk
1 Tb. smooth peanut butter
1 medium banana, sliced, or 1/2 Cup fresh or canned peaches or apricots

Combine all the ingredients in blender container. Blend for 30 to 60 seconds, until smooth. Serve in a tall glass.

Desserts

During treatment, some cancer patients lose all interest in sweets or even find the taste of sweets intolerable, while others develop a craving for sweets. When treatment ends, these altered conditions gradually return to normal.

The following recipes give you a choice of three kinds of desserts: nonsweet, semisweet, and sweet. If occasionally a dessert is all you wish to eat, that's all right since a sweet dessert is a good source of concentrated calories.

If you're cooking for yourself, these desserts are worth the effort, because dessert is a nice way of rewarding yourself for whatever you've accomplished during the day. When you are making a comeback from cancer, even the act of baking is an achievement, you realize.

If you're cooking for someone in the family who has cancer, the variety of desserts here can be shared and enjoyed by the whole family.

SAUTÉED BANANAS (NONSWEET)

One serving: 180 calories.

This recipe serves 2.

2 Tb. butter
2 firm, ripe bananas

Melt butter in a small skillet. Peel bananas and cut in half lengthwise. Sauté over moderate heat for about 5 minutes. Transfer to serving plate and spoon butter from pan over top. Dust with cinnamon, if you like. Serve warm.

To increase calories.
Two tablespoons heavy cream served over bananas will increase calories to 240.

Two tablespoons ice cream served with bananas will increase calories to 220.

SIMPLE BERRIES AND CREAM (NONSWEET)

Fast and easy.

One serving made with heavy cream: 150 calories, 1 gram protein.
One serving made with sour cream: 100 calories, 1 gram protein.

This recipe serves 1.

1/2 Cup fresh berries in season—strawberries, blueberries,
   raspberries, or other
2 Tb. heavy cream or sour cream

Place berries in chilled bowl. Top with cream or sour cream.

FRUIT COUPE   (NONSWEET)

One serving made with sour cream: 140 calories, 2 grams protein.
One serving made with yogurt: 103 calories, 13 grams protein.

This recipe serves 1.

2 Tb. sour cream or yogurt
1 Cup sliced fruit—any of the following are good with sour cream or yogurt:
   bananas, apples, prunes, grapes, apricots
OPTIONAL:
1 tsp. brown sugar
1 to 2 Tb. wheat germ

Blend sour cream or yogurt with sugar (if desired) in a small bowl.
Spoon over fruit. Sprinkle top with wheat germ. Try the coupe with and
without the sugar to see if you can tolerate the sweetness. To make a
thoroughly nonsweet dessert, use yogurt.

CINNAMON-ORANGE PRUNES (NONSWEET)

One cup: 290 calories, 2 grams protein.

This recipe serves 2 to 3.

1 orange
1 Tb. orange rind, julienne (cut into thin slices)
1/2 Cup orange juice
1 stick cinnamon
1 Cup pitted prunes
OPTIONAL:
2 tsp. brown sugar

Peel orange and save half of the rind. Scrape white pith from rind with small parring knife. Cut rind into thin slivers (julienne). Separate sections of orange.

Combine orange juice, julienned rind, cinnamon stick, prunes, and sugar, if desired, in a 1-quart saucepan. Heat to a gentle boil. Reduce heat and simmer slowly for 5 minutes. Remove from heat and add orange sections. Serve slightly warm or chilled. Can be refrigerated 4 to 5 days. Retain cinnamon stick, as it continues to add flavor.

To increase calories:
Two tablespoons ice cream served over the top will increase calories to 345 per cup.

Two tablespoons vanilla yogurt served over the top will increase calories to 331 per cup.

Two tablespoons orange liqueur poured over the top will increase calories to 335 per cup.

Two tablespoons heavy cream will increase calories to 410 per cup.

BLENDER APPLESAUCE   (NONSWEET)

A fresh-tasting applesauce you don't have to cook.

One-half cup: 60 calories.

This recipe makes 1 1/2 cups.

4 apples, cored and sliced
1 Tb. lemon juice
1 tsp. cinnamon
1 tsp. nutmeg
OPTIONAL:
2 tsp. honey or sugar (to taste)

Whir raw apple slices, skin and all, lemon juice, and cinnamon through blender. Sweeten with honey or sugar, if desired, to taste. The lemon juice will add tartness as well as preserving the color. Serve well chilled or at room temperature, dusted with nutmeg.

NOTE: If you don't have time to make your own applesauce, buy generic applesauce or natural-style applesauce. It isn't nearly as sweet as regular applesauce.

BROILED GRAPEFRUIT   (SEMISWEET)

One-half broiled grapefruit: 88 calories

This recipe makes 1/2 grapefruit.

1/2 grapefruit
1 tsp. brown sugar
1 tsp. butter, cut into slivers

Sprinkle grapefruit half with brown sugar. Arrange slivers of butter on top. Broil about four minutes. Can also be prepared without sugar.

BROILED GRAPEFRUIT WITH RUM

One-half broiled grapefruit: 104 calories.

This recipe makes 1/2 grapefruit.

Follow procedure for Broiled Grapefruit, but substitute 1 teaspoon rum for the brown sugar.

LEMON ICE   (SEMISWEET)

One-half cup: 117 calories, 3 grams protein.

This recipe makes slightly less than 3 cups.

1/2 Cup lemon juice
1/2 Cup sugar
Pinch of salt
2 Cups whole milk

Combine all ingredients and beat together in a medium-sized bowl. Place in freezer section of refrigerator and freeze in bowl until firm. Unchilled mixture may look as if it has curdled, but it will smooth during freezing. For an attractive presentation, serve in parfait glasses.

BAKED APPLES   (SEMISWEET)

One baked apple: 225 calories.

This recipe makes 4 baked apples.

4 large baking apples
1/4 Cup sugar or brown sugar
1 Tb. cinnamon
1/4 tsp. grated lemon rind
1/4 Cup (1/2 stick) butter or margarine, cut into small chunks
3/4 Cup water

Preheat oven to 350°. Wash apples and core to within 1/2 inch of bottom. Peel apples halfway down from top. Combine sugar, cinnamon, and lemon rind. Fill apple hollows with this mixture. Place apples upright in 8 x 8-inch pan, add water and dot apples with butter. Cover with heavy foil and bake at 350°, 45 minutes to 1 hour or until tender. After removing from oven, baste apples with pan juices. Serve warm or chilled.

To increase calories:
Two tablespoons cream served over top of 1 apple will increase calories to 285.

Two tablespoons ice cream served with 1 apple will increase calories to 265.

164

POACHED PEARS
MILANESE

(SEMISWEET)

One poached pear: 240 calories.

This recipe makes 4 poached pears.

4 small brown-skin pears
1 Cup domestic sauterne or any dry white wine
10 cloves
3 sticks cinnamon
1/2 Cup sugar

Preheat oven to 350°. Wash and drain pears. Core pears from bottom and trim bottoms so pears will stand upright—stems and leaves (if any) should be left on. Arrange pears in a deep casserole or saucepan, standing upright. In a small saucepan, bring wine, cinnamon, cloves, and sugar to a simmer. Pour simmering wine mixture over pears. Cover and poach in moderate 350° oven for 20 to 30 minutes. Serve warm or chilled with a little whipped cream or ice cream.

STOVE-TOP
RICE PUDDING   (SEMISWEET)

One-half cup: 155 calories, 6 grams protein.

This recipe makes 2 cups.

1 Cup water
1/2 Cup uncooked rice
1 egg, beaten
1/4 Cup sugar
Pinch of salt
3/4 Cup fortified milk*
1 tsp. vanilla
OPTIONAL:
1/4 Cup raisins

Heat water to boiling in a 2-quart saucepan. Stir in rice. Cover and lower heat. Simmer for about 10 minutes or until rice is cooked and all the water is absorbed. In the meantime, combine egg, sugar, salt, and milk. Add to cooked rice and mix well. Continue cooking over low heat until mixture thickens, about 5 minutes. Remove from heat; stir in vanilla and, if desired, raisins. Serve warm or chilled.

NOTE: Mixture tends to thicken if it stands for any length of time. If necessary, stir in additional milk or pour a little milk over each serving.

---

*To make fortified milk, mix 1 quart whole milk with 1 cup powdered skim milk.

LEMON SQUARES   (SEMISWEET)

Tart and moist.

One serving: 80 calories, 1 gram protein.

This recipe makes 16 servings.

CRUST:
1/2 Cup butter (1 stick), softened
1/4 Cup confectioners' sugar
1 Cup flour
FILLING:
2 eggs
1 Cup sugar
Juice and grated rind of 1 large lemon
1/2 tsp. baking soda
2 Tb. flour
Pinch of salt

CRUST: Preheat oven to 350°. Mix butter, confectioners' sugar, and flour in a large bowl until dough holds together smoothly. Pat evenly into the bottom of an 8 x 8-inch or 6 x 10-inch unbuttered glass baking dish. Bake at 350° for 25 to 30 minutes.

FILLING: While crust is baking, beat together eggs, sugar, lemon juice and rind, baking soda, flour, and salt in a medium-sized bowl. Pour over baked crust and return to 350° oven for 25 to 30 minutes. Cool completely before cutting into squares.

OLD-FASHIONED
STRAWBERRY SHORTCAKE (SEMISWEET)

Who can resist old-fashioned biscuit shortcakes, warm from the oven, split and buttered, covered with berries, and topped with lots of thick cream?

One strawberry shortcake: 400 calories, 6 grams protein.

This recipe makes 8 strawberry shortcakes.*

SHORTCAKE:
2 Cups all-purpose flour
1 Tb. baking powder
2 Tb. sugar
1/2 tsp. salt
6 Tb. butter
3/4 Cup milk
2 egg yolks
3 Tb. butter, softened to room
   temperature (to spread on biscuits
   when removed from oven)

STRAWBERRY MIX:
1 quart fresh (or frozen)
   strawberries**
CREAM TOPPING:
1 Cup heavy cream
1/2 tsp. vanilla

SHORTCAKE: Preheat oven to 425°. In a medium-sized bowl, mix together flour, baking powder, sugar, and salt. Add butter and either cut in with two kitchen knives or rub dry ingredients with butter between fingertips until mixture is consistency of coarse cornmeal. In a separate bowl, beat milk and egg yolks together with fork. Add to dry ingredients and mix lightly with fork until dough binds together. Drop dough off large spoon onto greased baking sheet to form 8 irregular mounds, spaced at least 2 inches apart. Bake at 425° for about 15 minutes or until tinged with brown.

---

*Unused shortcakes can be kept in your freezer for about one month. Or—toast split halves the next day and serve with butter and honey. Recipe can be cut in half to make four shortcakes instead of eight.

**Frozen or fresh sliced peaches and frozen or fresh raspberries may be used instead of strawberries.

168

STRAWBERRY MIX: Wash, hull, and either cut strawberries in half or slice. Toss with sugar, if desired. Do not let stand for more than a few hours.

CREAM TOPPING: Pour cream into a chilled, medium-sized mixing bowl. Whip at high speed with electric beater for one minute. Add vanilla and sugar, if desired. Continue whipping until cream is thick but still loose enough to run slowly off a spoon.

When shortcakes are done, let cool slightly. Split in half with a fork as you would an English muffin, and butter lightly. Cover bottom half of each shortcake with berries and some of their juice; add top half of shortcake. Spoon cream over all and garnish with a few more berries. Serve warm.

ENRICHED
COFFEE CAKE   (SEMISWEET)

This cake is moist and not too sweet.

One serving: 180 calories, 2 grams protein.

This recipe makes 16 servings.

CAKE:
1/2 Cup (1 stick) butter
1 Cup sugar
1 egg
1/2 Cup sour cream
1/2 tsp. vanilla
1/2 tsp. almond extract
1 Cup flour
2 Tb. soy flour
1/4 Cup nonfat powdered milk
1 tsp. baking powder
1/4 tsp. salt

TOPPING:
2 tsp. sugar
1/2 Cup chopped pecans
1 tsp. cinnamon

Preheat oven to 350°. Cream butter and sugar together in a medium-sized bowl. Add egg, sour cream, vanilla, and almond extract in that order. Add flours, powdered milk, baking powder, and salt. Mix until batter is smooth. In a separate bowl, combine sugar, nuts, and cinnamon. Pour one-third of the batter into a well-greased, lightly floured 8-inch-square pan. Sprinkle with three-fourths of nut mixture. Spoon in rest of batter. Sprinkle remaining nut mixture on top. Bake at 350° for 50 minutes.

ZABAGLIONE   (SWEET)

One-fourth cup: 145 calories, 4 grams protein.

This recipe makes 1/2 cup.

3 egg yolks
2 Tb. sugar
2 tsp. brandy or Marsala wine

Whip egg yolks, sugar, and brandy or Marsala together in a small bowl. Transfer mixture to top of double boiler over hot, but not boiling, water. Stir constantly with a wooden spoon until mixture thickens to a very heavy, creamlike consistency, about 3 to 5 minutes. Spoon into small custard cups and refrigerate until ready to serve.

CLASSIC SPONGE CAKE   (SWEET)

One slice: 130 calories, 4 grams protein.

This recipe makes 8 slices.

5 eggs, separated
1 Cup sugar
1 Tb. fresh lemon juice
Grated rind of 1/2 lemon
1/8 tsp. salt
1 Cup sifted flour

Preheat oven to 325°. Beat egg yolks in a medium-sized bowl until foamy. Gradually beat in sugar, lemon juice, and lemon rind and continue beating until thick.

In a separate bowl, beat egg whites vigorously until stiff peaks begin to form. Gently fold egg whites alternately with sifted flour into yolk mixture.

Line bottom of a 9-inch tube pan with wax paper cut to fit. Spoon batter into pan. Bake at 325° for 45 minutes. Invert pan on a cooling rack. Let cake cool completely before removing from pan.

Top with fresh fruit in season, if you wish.

COUNTRY POUND CAKE (SWEET)

One slice: 225 calories, 3 grams protein.

This recipe makes 1 large loaf (16 slices).

1 Cup (2 sticks) butter
1 Cup sugar
5 eggs

1 tsp. vanilla or brandy
2 Cups cake flour
1/8 tsp. salt

Preheat oven to 325°. Cream butter and sugar together until light and fluffy. Beat in eggs, one at a time, and continue beating until batter is smooth and creamy. Add vanilla or brandy. Gradually add flour and salt, blending until smooth. Spoon batter into buttered and lightly floured 9 x 5 x 3-inch loaf pan. Bake at 325° for 1 hour. Flavor improves and slicing is easier after cake has "set" for a day. Cake freezes well— wrap individual slices in plastic wrap or foil so that you can defrost 1 or 2 slices at a time. Serve with butter, jam, ice cream, or Strawberry Cream Topping (page 115).

QUICK LEMON POUND CAKE

One half-inch slice: 350 calories, 4 grams protein.

This recipe makes 1 large loaf (16 slices).

1 box (16 oz. or 17 oz.) pound cake mix
2 to 3 eggs, depending upon what
   pound cake mix instructions call for

3/4 Cup sour cream
2 Tb. grated lemon rind
2 Tb. lemon juice

Preheat oven to 325°. Prepare pound cake mix according to package directions, using sour cream instead of milk. Add lemon rind and lemon juice to batter. Pour into a well-greased 9 x 5 x 3-inch loaf pan. Bake at 325° for 1 1/2 hours or until top is golden brown. Cool on wire rack (cooled cake slices easily). Top with fresh strawberries, if in season.

ITALIAN FRUIT TORTE (SWEET)

One slice: 280 calories, 4 grams protein.

This recipe makes 12 slices.

CRUST:
1/2 Cup (1 stick) sweet (unsalted) butter
1 Cup flour
5 Tb. sugar
FILLING:
3 Cups of your favorite fruit or fruits, fresh, canned, or stewed
1/2 Cup chopped nuts
TOPPING:
3 eggs
1 Cup sugar
1/3 Cup flour
1/4 tsp. vanilla
1 tsp. baking powder
1/2 tsp. cinnamon

CRUST: Preheat oven to 350°. Cut butter into small pieces. Using fingers, mix butter, flour, and sugar together until mixture becomes soft and doughlike. Press into an 8-inch round cake or spring-form pan. Bake at 350° for 20 minutes. Remove from oven and let cool for a few minutes.

FILLING: Layer 3 cups of your favorite fruit or fruits over crust. Try peaches, plums, apricots, apples, or a combination of fruit (plums and apricots are especially good). Top with any kind of nuts—walnuts, pecans, or almonds, for example.

TOPPING: Beat eggs, sugar, flour, vanilla, baking powder, and cinnamon together until light and fluffy. Pour egg mixture over crust and fruit. Be sure to spread egg mixture evenly over entire torte. Return to oven and bake at 350° another 30 minutes.

OLD-FASHIONED APPLE CAKE   (SWEET)

An exceptionally moist cake.

One slice: 575 calories, 7 grams protein.

This recipe makes 12 slices.

3 Cups flour
1 tsp. baking soda
2 tsp. cinnamon
1/4 tsp. salt
3 eggs
1 1/2 Cups vegetable oil
2 Cups sugar
2 tsp. vanilla
3 Cups pared, cored, thickly sliced apples (4 medium cooking apples)
1 Cup chopped walnuts

Preheat oven to 350°. In a large bowl, mix flour, baking soda, cinnamon, and salt. In another large bowl, beat eggs, oil, and sugar together until light and fluffy. Gradually mix in dry ingredients. Add vanilla. Batter will be stiff. Fold in the apples and the nuts. Turn into a lightly greased 9-inch tube or bundt pan. Bake at 350° for 1 1/2 hours—or until toothpick inserted into center of cake comes out clean.

ORANGE-GLAZED CAKE (SWEET)

One slice: 360 calories, 4 grams protein.

This recipe makes 10 slices.

1 Cup (2 sticks) butter or margarine
3 eggs
1 Cup sugar
2 Cups flour
1 Tb. baking powder
2 oranges
1 lemon
1/2 Cup confectioners' sugar

Preheat oven to 350°. Beat butter or margarine, eggs, and sugar together until light and fluffy. Gradually add flour and baking powder. Beat until smooth. Batter will be fairly stiff. Spread evenly into a greased and lightly floured, round, 9-inch tube or bundt pan. Bake at 350° for 45 minutes or until cake is a light golden brown.

While cake is baking, prepare the juice mixture. Grate the skin of one orange and one lemon. Add grated rind to juice of two oranges and one lemon. Mix well with confectioners' sugar.

As soon as cake is done, remove from oven and prick holes evenly over the entire cake with a fork. Immediately pour or spoon juice mixture over cake until liquid is completely absorbed. Top with strawberries or orange slices if you wish. A refreshing change of pace.

BRANDY BALLS   (SWEET)

One brandy ball: 60 calories, 1 gram protein.

This recipe makes about 25 brandy balls.

2 Cups crushed vanilla wafers (about 40 wafers)
1 Cup walnuts, finely ground
2 Tb. corn syrup
1/4 to 1/3 Cup brandy or rum, to taste
1/3 Cup confectioners' sugar

Process wafers and walnuts by putting them in a blender container and blending until a fine crumb is reached—or place wafers and walnuts inside a double plastic bag, tie off end, and crush with rolling pin.

Combine crumbs, walnuts, corn syrup, and liquor in a medium-sized bowl. Mix well and shape into small, firm balls about 3/4-inch in diameter. Roll each ball in confectioners' sugar. Store in jar or tin with lid. Flavor improves with age.

LITTLE CHEESECAKES   (SWEET)

One cupcake: 170 calories, 3 1/2 grams protein.

This recipe makes 6 cupcakes.

1 package (8 oz.) cream cheese, softened
1/3 Cup sugar
1 egg
1 tsp. vanilla

Preheat oven to 375°. Beat softened cream cheese in a medium-sized bowl until light and fluffy. Add sugar, egg, and vanilla. Mix thoroughly.

Line a 6-cup muffin tin with paper liners. Fill each cup 3/4 full with batter. Bake at 375° for 30 minutes or until cupcakes test done (knife inserted into center of cupcake should come out clean). Cool on rack. Can be eaten plain or topped with sweetened strawberries or any other fruit in season.

APPLE-NUT SQUARES (SWEET)

One square: 85 calories, 2 grams protein.

This recipe makes 9 squares.

1 egg
1/3 Cup sugar
2 Tb. all-purpose flour
1 1/4 tsp. baking powder
1 tsp. vanilla
1/2 Cup chopped walnuts
1/2 Cup chopped apple (1 medium apple) pared and cored

Preheat oven to 350°. Beat egg and sugar together until smooth and creamy. Blend in flour, baking powder, and vanilla. Stir in nuts and apple. Spoon into a greased and lightly floured 8 x 8-inch pan. Bake at 350° for 30 minutes. Serve warm or cold.

To increase calories:
Two tablespoons ice cream served over top will increase calories to 165 per square.

Two tablespoons vanilla yogurt served over top will increase calories to 151 per square.

Two tablespoons whipped cream served over top will increase calories to 225 per square.

GINGERSNAPS   (SWEET)

A traditional Christmas favorite.

One cookie: 65 calories, 1 gram protein.

This recipe makes about 4 dozen.

3/4 Cup butter (1 1/2 stick)
1/3 Cup dark molasses
1 egg
1 Cup sugar
1 1/2 Cups flour
1/2 Cup soy flour
1 Tb. baking soda
Pinch of salt
1 tsp. ginger
1 tsp. cinnamon
1 tsp. ground cloves

Preheat oven to 375   Cream butter, molasses, egg, and sugar together. Slowly add flours, baking soda, and spices.

Form dough into small balls and roll in a small bowl of sugar to coat. Place on greased cookie sheet and bake at 375° for 12 to 15 minutes.

GERMAN ALMOND SLICES
(MANDELBROT)
(SWEET)

An authentic German sweetbread.

One slice (1/2 inch): 70 calories, 2 grams protein.

This recipe makes 15 to 20 slices.

1 egg
1/3 Cup sugar
2 Tb. oil
2 Tb. chopped almonds
1/4 tsp. almond or vanilla extract
1/2 Tb. grated lemon rind
1 Cup flour
1 Tb. baking powder

Preheat oven to 350°. In a medium-sized bowl, beat egg and sugar together until light and fluffy. Stir in remaining ingredients, adding flour and baking powder last. Continue stirring to form a soft dough.

Turn out dough onto well-floured board or table. Rub hands with a small amount of flour to keep dough from sticking to hands. Roll and pat dough with your hands to shape a long loaf, about 3 inches wide and 3/4-inch thick. Slip long loaf onto greased baking sheet. Bake at 350° for 35 minutes. With a serrated bread knife, cut into 1/2-inch-thick slices while still warm.

WHOLE WHEAT SUGAR COOKIES   (SWEET)

One cookie: 82 calories, 1 gram protein.

This recipe makes 2 to 3 dozen cookies.

1 Cup sugar
1 tsp. baking powder
1/8 tsp. salt
1/2 tsp. baking soda
1/2 tsp. nutmeg
1/2 Cup butter or margarine, softened
2 Tb. milk
2 Tb. grated lemon or orange peel
1 tsp. vanilla
1 egg
2 Cups whole wheat flour
2 Tb. sugar
1/2 tsp. cinnamon

Preheat oven to 375°. Combine first 10 ingredients in a large bowl. Blend well. To measure flour, lightly spoon into a measuring cup and level off. Stir in flour. Shape mixture into 1-inch balls. Place on ungreased cookie sheets 2 inches apart. Flatten slightly with back of spoon. Combine sugar and cinnamon and sprinkle over cookies. Bake at 375° for 8 to 10 minutes, until a light golden brown. Cookies will be soft in the center and are delightful with a fragrant cup of hot tea.

Beer, Wine, and Other Drinks

Some cancer patients in treatment cannot tolerate either the taste or effects of alcohol. Others find that a light drink before eating stimulates their appetites and that a glass of wine at lunch or dinner enhances meals. At other times, the slight "bite" of cold beer can be very appealing.

If 80-proof alcohol is simply too strong, stick to beer or wine or try aperitifs, such as Dubonnet or Campari. On a cold gray day, Mulled Wine or Mulled Cider is warming and companionable. On a sleepless night, a little brandy in a glass of warmed milk is comforting and may even induce drowsiness.

Cancer patients taking strong pain medication or tranquilizers must check with their physicians to learn whether alcohol will interact badly with their drugs. Patients using THC or marijuana to lessen nausea and vomiting must also check with their doctors on the risks of interaction with alcohol.

Alcohol has virtually nothing to offer as a source of protein, but it can provide useful calories:

	CALORIES	GRAMS PROTEIN
Gin, Rum, Vodka, Scotch, Bourbon, Brandy		
80 proof, 1 1/2 fl. oz. = 1 jigger	95	0
Wines, Table		
12% alcohol, 3 1/2 fl. oz.	85	0
Wines, Sweet		
18% alcohol, 3 1/2 fl. oz.		
Sherry, Campari, Dubonnet, Port	140	0
Beer, 4.5% alcohol, 12 fl. oz.	150	1

COCKTAILS AND BAR DRINKS
An old bartender's trick: if you like your drinks over ice and *cold*, vigorous stirring will intensify the coldness and chill the glass as well.

Gin and Tonic (165 calories)
   6 to 8 oz. tonic water (to taste)
   1 jigger gin

Stir tonic water and gin with ice in highball glass.

Hot Toddy (110 calories)
   Place 1 teaspoon of sugar in a mug.
   Add 1 cup boiling water, 1 jigger Scotch or Bourbon and stir.

Scotch and Milk (225 calories)
   1 cup milk
   1 jigger Scotch (or 1 jigger brandy or bourbon)

Warm milk in small saucepan. Stir in Scotch. Serve immediately in thick mug.

Whiskey Sour   (110 calories)
   Juice of 1/2 lemon
   1 tsp. sugar
   1 jigger Bourbon or other whiskey

Blend ingredients in blender or shake together with ice until
frothy. Strain into tall glass over ice. Garnish with orange
slice and cherry.

Screwdriver   (175 calories)
   8 oz. orange juice
   1 jigger vodka

Place three ice cubes, vodka, and orange juice in highball
glass. Stir rigorously. Garnish with orange slice.

Bloody Mary   (130 calories)
   8 oz. tomato juice
   1 jigger vodka
   1 Tb. fresh lemon juice
   Salt and pepper to taste
   OPTIONAL:
   1 dash Worcestershire sauce
   2 drops Tabasco or
   2 drops Pickapeppa

Place 3 or 4 ice cubes in a tall 10-oz. glass. Add lemon juice
and any of the optional ingredients. Add salt and pepper. Stir
in vodka and, lastly, the tomato juice with a celery stick.

Cranberry Cocktail   (260 calories)
   1 Cup cranberry juice cocktail
   1 Tb. lemon juice
   1/8 tsp. nutmeg
   1 jigger brandy

Mix all ingredients and serve on ice in a tall glass; garnish
with lemon wedge.

Mulled Wine   (105 calories)
   3 1/2 oz. red wine
   2 sticks cinnamon
   1 or 2 whole cloves

Warm slowly in a small saucepan over low heat for 5 minutes.
Remove cinnamon and cloves. Serve warm in a thick mug.

Mulled Cider   (150 calories)
   1 Cup apple cider
   2 sticks cinnamon
   2 or 3 whole cloves
   1 Tb. brandy

Warm slowly in a small saucepan over low heat for 5 minutes.
Remove cinnamon and cloves. Serve warm in a thick mug.

IIII

NUTRITIONAL SAVVY: WHAT NOBODY ELSE TELLS YOU

Nutritional Goals

Though there is no question that cancer and its treatment damage body tissues, the losses need not be permanent. Solid research, conducted at medical centers, shows that diets high in protein and calories not only repair tissues but help cancer patients tolerate the side effects of treatment. Continuing research now indicates that patients who maintain their weight may even be capable of accepting higher doses of treatment.

During treatment (which is often enervating), every cancer patient's protein needs nearly double and his calorie needs increase 20 percent. Protein is consumed so much more rapidly at this time that extra calories (which act like a buffer) are needed to keep protein from being used solely for energy, with nothing leftover for tissue repair.

How to calculate your protein and calorie needs
Protein Needs

Healthy adults need approximately .36*grams of protein per pound of desirable weight every day. Cancer patients who have lost weight need approximately one gram of protein per pound of desirable weight. Your physician will tell you what weight is desirable for you at this stage. Use .9 as the factor to calculate your protein needs, i.e., multiply your desired weight by .9. There are no absolutes as height/weight charts suggest because desirable weight is based on a variety of factors—your height, your age, your bone structure, your metabolic rate.

If your doctor says your desirable weight is 125 pounds, then you'll need 112 grams of protein daily. Similarly, if your desirable weight is 175 pounds, then 157 grams of protein per day will be what you need.
Calorie Needs:

A cancer patient who has lost weight should multiply his desirable weight (in pounds) by 20** to arrive at his minimum calorie needs.

If your doctor says your desirable weight is 125 pounds, then you'll need 2,500 calories daily. Similarly, if your desirable weight is 175 pounds, then 3,500 calories per day will be what you need.

---

*Food and Nutrition Board, National Academy of Sciences. The National Research Council: Recommended Dietary Allowances. Ninth Edition 1980, Washington, DC

** Source: Blackburn, George, M.D.; Bistrian, Bruce R., M.D.; Maini, Baltej S., M.D.; Schlamm, Haran T.; Smith, Michael, M.D., "Nutritional and Metabolic Assessment of the Hospitalized Patient," *Journal of Parenteral and Enteral Nutrition,* Volume 1, No. 1, p. 15, 1977.

Right now, you may not be able to eat enough to reach your desirable amounts of protein and calories, but do your best each day, taking advantage of the days you feel well to eat more. On these days, try to eat foods especially rich in protein and calories.

Other Nutrients

Carbohydrates, fats, minerals (calcium and iron), and vitamins also play important roles:

NUTRIENT	FUNCTION
Carbohydrates	Provide calories, minerals, and vitamins.
Fats and Oils	Supply a rich source of calories in small amounts. Dairy fats (sour cream, whipping cream) also supply calcium.
Calcium	Important to bone and teeth formation and strength. Calcium also aids blood clotting and muscle contraction.
Iron	Needed to make hemoglobin (the oxygen-carrying substance in blood). Prevents anemia and the fatigue which can result from anemia. Increases resistance to infection.
Vitamin A	Helps maintain normal night vision. Also offers protection against infection.
Vitamin B Complex The most important B vitamins are Thiamine (B1), Riboflavin (B2), Niacin, Folacin, Pyridoxine (B6), and Vitamin B12.	
Thiamine (B1)	Aids digestion. Helps nervous system function properly.
Riboflavin (B2)	Creates usable energy from carbohydrates and protein.

189

NUTRIENT	FUNCTION
Niacin	Puts carbohydrates to use as energy. Helps digestive processes.
Folacin and Vitamin B12	Needed for the manufacture of red blood cells.
Pyridoxine (B6)	Important to maintenance of a healthy nervous system.
Vitamin C	Helps with wound healing; also offers protection against infection.
Vitamin D	Important to bone formation and bone strength.

If you eat a variety of foods, your diet is well balanced. However, if your eating habits tend to be one-sided, say you never eat fruits or vegetables or you never drink milk, some changes would be helpful. A well-balanced diet should include at least one serving a day from each of the following categories (the recipes in this book combine many of them for you, but it's up to you to do some simple menu planning).

Meat, Fish, Poultry, Eggs, Nuts, Beans

These are your primary sources of protein, iron, and B-vitamins. Some examples:

Three ounces of pork contain 21 grams of protein, 2.5 milligrams of iron, .45 milligrams of thiamine, .21 milligrams of riboflavin, and 4.4 milligrams of niacin.

Three ounces of solid white tuna contain 25 grams of protein, 1.5 milligrams of iron, a trace of thiamine, .10 milligrams of riboflavin, and 13 milligrams of niacin.

Three ounces of chicken contain 25 grams of protein, 1.7 milligrams of iron, .05 milligrams of thiamine, .18 milligrams of riboflavin, and .90 milligrams of niacin.

One large egg contains 6.5 grams of protein, 1.2 milligrams of iron, .05 milligrams of thiamine, .15 milligrams of riboflavin, and a trace of niacin.

To weigh small amounts of food, buy any scale that accurately measures grams and ounces.

Breads, Grains, Cereals, Pasta, Waffles, Pancakes

These provide essential carbohydrates, iron, and B-vitamins. When planning menus, remember that rice and cornmeal are grains and that baked goods are part of this group too.

Some examples:

One slice of bread contains 14 grams of carbohydrate, .70 milligrams of iron, .07 milligrams of thiamine, .06 milligrams of riboflavin, and .70 milligrams of niacin.

One-half cup of spaghetti contains 16 grams of carbohydrate, .70 milligrams of iron, .10 milligrams of thiamine, .06 milligrams of riboflavin, and .80 milligrams of niacin.

A 4 1/2 x 4 1/2-inch waffle contains 18 grams of carbohydrate, .9 milligrams of iron, .09 milligrams of thiamine, .13 milligrams of riboflavin, and .70 milligrams of niacin.

Milk, Cream, Whipping Cream, Ice Cream, Yogurt, Sour Cream, Cheese

These supply protein, calcium, vitamin A, and vitamin D. Milk or cream used in cooked foods (sauces, cream soups, custards, cakes) can count toward filling your daily needs in this group.

Some examples:

One cup of whole milk contains 8 grams of protein, 288 milligrams of calcium, 350 I.U. (International Units) of vitamin A, and 100 I.U. of vitamin D.

One cup of ice cream contains 6 grams of protein, 194 milligrams of calcium, 590 I.U. of vitamin A, and 66 I.U. of vitamin D.

One ounce of Cheddar cheese contains 7 grams of protein, 213 milligrams of calcium, 370 I.U. of vitamin A, and 75 I.U. of vitamin D.

Fruits and Vegetables

These are important sources of vitamin A, vitamin C, potassium, and fiber. Fiber, although not a nutrient, helps in regulating bowel movements.

Some examples:

One medium orange contains 260 I.U. of vitamin A, 66 milligrams of vitamin C, and 263 milligrams of potassium.

One medium banana contains 230 I.U. of vitamin A, 12 milligrams of vitamin C, and 444 milligrams of potassium.

One medium raw carrot contains 7,930 I.U. of vitamin A, 6 milligrams of vitamin C, and 246 milligrams of potassium.

Fats and Oils

Since fats have double the calories, gram per gram, of protein or carbohydrates, they are a marvelous concentrated source of calories. Butter, margarine, cream, sour cream, mayonnaise, chicken fat, bacon fat, and cooking and salad oils are all included in this group. If your appetite is poor, this is not the time to worry about your cholesterol level; weight maintenance is paramount. What's most essential is that you eat as well as possible, concentrating on foods rich in protein and calories.

The Vitamin Craze

Many quack diets claim that megadoses of vitamins are a cure-all for cancer. Yet, to date, there is *no* scientific evidence to show that large amounts of vitamins affect cancer in any way, let alone cure it. In fact, megadose vitamin diets can do serious harm and can even be fatal.

If you eat a variety of foods you should automatically supply your daily vitamin requirements. Vitamin supplements are not recommended unless prescribed by a physician.

Protein Complementing

Complete protein, which is found only in meat, fowl, fish, eggs, and dairy products, contains 22 amino acids. Eight of these—the essential amino acids*—are crucial in making new protein but all 22 are necessary to the human body for repair of blood, muscle, and skin. Incomplete protein is low in one or more of the essential amino acids.

Protein complementing is simply a way of combining foods that have incomplete protein to make complete protein. For example, peanut butter contains incomplete protein and so does bread. But if the two are combined in a peanut butter sandwich, the incomplete protein of the peanut butter and the bread complement each other and give complete (whole) protein.

The complete protein of eggs and dairy products also complements and upgrades the incomplete protein of grain and legumes (beans and peas). Combine bread with eggs and milk, as in Baked French Toast (page 33), and you get six grams of complete protein.

Here are some examples of how incomplete protein combinations are completed in recipes in this book:

Incomplete Sources	Complete Sources	Protein-Rich Recipe
Peanut butter	+ milk	Old Colony Peanut Soup (page 93)
Potatoes	+ milk	Potato Soup (page 94)
Noodles	+ cottage cheese	Kugel (page 37)
Kidney beans and tortillas	+ cheese	Bean and Cheese Tortilla (page 70)
Peanut butter and flour	+ egg	Peanut Butter Muffins (page 81)
Chick peas and bread or crackers		Armenian Hommus Dip (page 13)

---

*Leucine, isoleucine, threonine, valine, lysine, methionine, phenylalanine, and tryptophan.

More Protein and Calorie Boosters

Because cancer patients may have trouble gaining or maintaining weight, foods that are especially high in protein and calories provide a particularly significant nutritional resource. Especially useful are the foods listed here, which add extra calories and protein without increasing food bulk or volume.

Boosting Protein

—Two tablespoons of powdered milk provide 3 grams of protein. Nonfat dry milk is one of the most convenient protein boosters as it can easily be added to all kinds of baked goods, sauces, hot cereal, egg dishes, or beverages.

—Regular whole milk can be fortified—or made into double-strength milk—by adding powdered, nonfat dry milk. The volume is not changed, yet the protein in each cup of milk is almost doubled.

One quart of whole milk plus one cup of nonfat dry milk produces one quart of double-strength milk. One cup of double-strength milk contains 220 calories and 15 grams of protein. Thorough chilling improves the flavor markedly.

—Use milk, double-strength or evaporated, in place of water when making soups or hot cereals. Add extra ice cream to milkshakes. Or, make a root beer float (Black Cow) for 235 calories and 2 grams protein.

One packet of instant breakfast powder mixed with 8 ounces of whole milk provides 280 calories and 15 grams of protein, while one packet mixed with one cup of double-strength milk gives 340 calories and 21 grams of protein.

—One ounce of grated cheese supplies 7 grams of protein and can be added to sauces or sprinkled over casseroles or vegetables.

—Two tablespoons of soy flour contain 6 grams of protein and can be added to the flour called for in bread, cake, or cookie recipes. It should be used sparingly, however, since it has a strong flavor.

—Tofu, oriental soybean curd, now available in many supermarkets, has a bland flavor but excellent protein. Cut into squares, use in clear broth. One 2-inch square gives you 9 grams protein and 85 calories.

—One egg offers 6.5 grams of protein. Finely chopped hard-boiled eggs can be added to sauces or salads. Choose desserts or baked goods made with eggs.

Boosting Calories

—One teaspoon of butter or margarine adds 35 calories and can be used in any number of ways. Stir butter or margarine into soups; drizzle melted butter or margarine over cooked cereal or vegetables; warm bread and rolls so that extra butter or margarine is absorbed. For variety and for added flavor, save bacon drippings and use in place of butter on vegetables (one teaspoon of bacon fat adds 35 calories). All fats are concentrated sources of calories; use them liberally in preparing and serving foods.

—One tablespoon of mayonnaise offers 100 calories. Use mayonnaise in salads, deviled eggs, and as a spread for Danish sandwiches.

—Two tablespoons of sour cream provide 60 calories and can be served over vegetables or fruits and in sauces or dips.

—Two tablespoons of heavy (whipping) cream contain 100 calories. Use as a topping for ice cream; stewed, canned, or fresh fruits; or cake.

—Two tablespoons of powdered, nondairy creamer give 60 calories and can be added to soups, sauces, milkshakes, or hot cereal without adding volume.

—Polycose, a commercial calorie supplement available in most drugstores, comes in liquid or powdered form. Once opened, the liquid form must be used within 24 hours but the powdered form can be stored in a dry place indefinitely. Polycose is almost tasteless and adds no extra volume. If you need its extra calories, keep it on your kitchen counter so that you remember to use it each time you prepare food or beverages. Since 1 tablespoon of powdered Polycose contains 32 calories and one ounce of the liquid contains 60 calories, regular use can add up to a significant calorie count.

Label Reading

Knowing how to read and interpret the information on labels of canned and packaged foods can be invaluable in calculating daily nutritional intake.

Most labels list the number of calories and the grams of protein, carbohydrates, and fats provided by a serving of a specified amount of food. Also included are the per-serving percentages of the minimum daily requirements (U.S. RDA—United States Recommended Daily Allowances, established by the federal Food and Drug Administration) of protein, vitamins, and minerals for healthy adults. Since cancer patients need nearly 50 percent more protein and 20 percent more calories daily than healthy individuals, the percentages on the labels must be adjusted, but they do at least provide a starting point.

Here is a typical label from an eight-ounce carton of small curd cottage cheese:

SMALL CURD COTTAGE CHEESE, 8 OUNCES

Nutrition information per serving

Serving size	4 oz.	Protein	14 Grams
Servings per container	2	Carbohydrates	4 Grams
Calories	120	Fats	5 Grams

Percentage of the U.S. Recommended Daily Allowances (U.S. RDA)

Protein	30%	Niacin	*
Vitamin A	4%	Calcium	6%
Vitamin C	*	Iron	*
Thiamine	*	Vitamin B12	15%
Riboflavin	10%	Phosphorus	15%

*Contains less than 2% of the U.S. RDA.

To translate these vitamin and mineral percentages into more common units of measurement (e.g., milligrams of calcium or iron), refer to the U.S. Recommended Daily Allowances given.

U.S. Recommended Daily Allowances (U.S. RDA)*

Vitamins, Minerals, and Protein	Unit of Measurement	Healthy Adults and Healthy Children 4 or More Years of Age
Vitamin A	International Units	5,000
Vitamin D	International Units	400
Vitamin E	International Units	30
Vitamin C	Milligrams	60
Folic Acid	Milligrams	0.4
Thiamine	Milligrams	1.5
Riboflavin	Milligrams	1.7
Niacin	Milligrams	20
Vitamin B 6	Milligrams	2.0
Vitamin B 12	Micrograms	6.0
Biotin	Milligrams	0.3
Pantothenic Acid	Milligrams	10
Calcium	Grams	1.0
Phosphorus	Grams	1.0
Iodine	Micrograms	150
Iron	Milligrams	18
Magnesium	Milligrams	400
Copper	Milligrams	2.0
Zinc	Milligrams	15
Protein	Grams	45

Food labels also list all ingredients according to ingredient weight, with the dominant ingredient listed first and the rest in descending order.

At present, federal law requires labeling only for foods that have had nutrients added, or have promoted specific claims, e.g., "you get double your Vitamin C daily minimum requirement", or are for a specific dietary use like dietetic or low cholesterol foods.

---

*U.S. DEPARTMENT OF HEALTH, EDUCATION, AND WELFARE: Public Health Service: Food and Drug Administration.

From the Supermarket

The table below lists the protein and calories of more than 100 supermarket products:

	Portion Size 1 cup = 8 oz.	Protein (Grams)	Calories
DAIRY			
Milk, whole	1 cup	8	160
2%	1 cup	8	120
skim	1 cup	8	80
chocolate	1 cup	8	200
buttermilk	1 cup	9	85
Cream, half & half	2 Tb.	1	40
light or table	2 Tb.	1	65
heavy or whipping	2 Tb.	1	105
sour	2 Tb.	1	56
Butter	1 Tb.	—	100
Margarine	1 Tb.	—	100
Ice Cream	1 cup	4	260
Yogurt, plain	1 cup	12	150
fruit	1 cup	10	260
Cheese, Cheddar	1 slice	4	70
Swiss	1 slice	4	70
Brick	1 slice	4	70
American	1 slice	4	70
BEVERAGES			
Instant breakfast powders All flavors	1 package plus 8 oz. whole milk	15	280
Flavored coffees	8 oz.	1	80
Eggnog	8 oz.	11	270
Hot chocolate	8 oz.	12	270
Ovaltine	8 oz.	12	270
Soda pop, cola	8 oz.	—	95
ginger ale	8 oz.	—	75
HI C	8 oz.	—	120
Fruit juices, apple	8 oz.	—	115
cranberry	8 oz.	—	140

	Portion Size 1 cup = 8 oz.	Protein (Grams)	Calories
BEVERAGES (continued)			
Fruit juices, grape	8 oz.	—	160
mango/pineapple	8 oz.	—	190
prune	8 oz.	—	150
orange	8 oz.	—	120
tomato	8 oz.	—	45
GRAIN PRODUCTS			
Breads, English muffin	1	4	140
crescent roll	1	2	130
corn bread	2" square	3	130
raisin bread	1 slice	2	75
sweet roll/Danish	1	2	160
date-nut	1 slice	2	65
dinner roll	1	1	65
Cereals, cold			
Kelloggs Concentrate	1/3 cup	12	110
Special K	1/3 cup	6	110
Life	1/3 cup	3	60
granola	1/4 cup	3	130
Cereals, hot			
oatmeal (instant)	1 package	4	105-175
oatmeal (regular)	1/2 cup	2	65
farina	1/2 cup	2	65
cream of wheat, rice, Wheatena, Malt-O-Meal	1/2 cup	2	60
Cakes (mixes)			
banana	1 slice	2	120
brownie	2" square	1	120
devil's food	2" wedge	3	200
gingerbread	2" square	1	180
white	2" wedge	3	200
Misc., Rice-A-Roni	1/2 cup	2	65
stuffing	1/2 cup	3	160
croutons	1/4 cup	3	120
Shake & Bake coating	1/4 pkg.	2	70
macaroni & cheese	1/2 cup	8	225
crepe, filled with 3 Tb. creamed chicken	1	7	160

199

	Portion Size 1 cup = 8 oz.	Protein (Grams)	Calories
SNACK FOODS			
Granola Bars	1	2	110
Breakfast Bars	1 plus 8 oz. whole milk	14	360
Breakfast Squares	2	12	380
Figurines	2	11	275
Potato chips	15-20	2	150
Chow mein noodles	1/2 cup	3	110
Pretzels	1/2 cup	3	100
Sesame sticks	1/2 cup	6	300
Potato sticks	1/2 cup	1	95
Crackers, Saltines	2 squares	1	28
Ritz	2	1	34
Fritos	1/2 cup	1	115
Bacos	2 Tb.	4	80
SOUPS			
Beef or Chicken noodle	1 cup	4	75
Clam chowder, Manhattan	1 cup	1	80
New England	1 cup	9	160
Cream of mushroom	1 cup	1	150
Split pea	1 cup	8	170
Vegetable beef	1 cup	4	75
(Combine soups to create new flavors too)			
FRUITS AND VEGETABLES			
Fruits; frozen, strawberries, peaches, blueberries	1/2 cup	—	40
canned, applesauce	1/2 cup	—	115
peaches, in heavy syrup	1/2 cup	—	95
pineapple, in heavy syrup	2 rings	—	85
fruit cocktail	1/2 cup	—	95
dried, raisins	2 Tb.	2	50
prunes	5	2	75
apricots	5	2	50

200

	Portion Size 1 cup = 8 oz.	Protein (Grams)	Calories
FRUITS AND VEGETABLES (continued)			
Vegetables; frozen			
broccoli with cheese sauce	1/2 cup	4	120
green peas with			
cream sauce	1/2 cup	4	130
creamed spinach	1/2 cup	3	80
potato puffs	5	2	100
lima beans in butter			
sauce	1/2 cup	5	110
creamed corn	1/2 cup	2	90
Hawaiian style vegetables	1/2 cup	1	100
MEAT ENTREES			
Beef pot pie	8 oz.	16	410
Lasagna with meat	6 oz.	10	260
Chili with meat	6 oz.	11	240
Meat ravioli	6 oz.	7	175
Corned beef hash	4 oz.	9	205
Veal Parmagian	6 oz.	11	230
Spaghetti and meatballs	6 oz.	6	215
DELI DEPARTMENT			
Salads, macaroni	1/2 cup	5	203
potato	1/2 cup	4	180
slaw	1/2 cup	3	112
fruit with sour cream and			
coconut	1/2 cup	2	175
baked beans	1/2 cup	6	130
Desserts, tapioca	1/2 cup	3	150
vanilla pudding	1/2 cup	3	160
coconut cream pie	2" wedge	7	270
apple pie with a slice			
of Cheddar cheese	2" wedge	10	375
blueberry pie	2" wedge	3	286
blueberry pie a la mode	2" wedge	6	415
cheesecake	2" wedge	7	350
Meats: see pages 139-40			

Carry-Out Foods

There's nothing wrong with a McDonald's quarter-pounder with cheese or an order of chicken chow mein with Chinese noodles when you don't feel like cooking. Most carry-out foods provide more nutrition than people realize. For example, a McDonald's quarter-pounder with cheese contains 520 calories and 31 grams of protein, while a half-pint order of chicken chow mein with one-half cup of Chinese noodles offers 285 calories and 12 grams of protein.

The protein and calorie values of the following Carry-Out Foods were computed by the West Suburban Dietetic Association of Illinois.

	Portion Size	Protein (Grams)	Calories
ARTHUR TREACHER'S FISH & CHIPS, INC.			
Chicken	2 pieces	27.1	369
Chicken sandwich	1	16.2	413
Chips	25	4	276
Chowder	3/4 cup	4.6	112
Coleslaw	1/2 cup	1	123
Fish	2 pieces	19.2	355
Fish sandwich	1	16.4	440
Shrimp	7 pieces	13.1	381
BURGER KING			
Cheeseburger	1	17	305
French Fries	25	3	214
Hamburger	1	14	252
Hot dog	1	11	291
Vanilla shake	1	11	332
Whopper	1	29	606

	Portion Size	Protein (Grams)	Calories
DAIRY QUEEN			
Big Brazier, deluxe	1	28	470
regular	1	27	457
with cheese	1	32	553
French fries, small order	small	2	200
large order	large	3	320
Chocolate dipped cone	medium	7	300
Chocolate malt	medium	15	600
Chocolate sundae	medium	6	300
Cone	medium	6	230
Freeze	1	11	520
Parfait	1	10	460
Frozen Dairy, banana split	1	10	540
fiesta sundae	1	9	570
Mr. Misty Float	1	6	440
Mr. Misty Freeze	1	10	500
KENTUCKY FRIED CHICKEN			
Dinners (with mashed potatoes,			
coleslaw, roll, etc.)—extra crispy		52	950
original recipe		52	830
Individual pieces—original recipe			
drumsticks	1	14	136
rib (1/2 breast)	1	19	241
thigh	1	20	276
wing	1	11	151
LONG JOHN SILVER'S, INC.			
Clams with batter	1 order	13.3	465
Corn on the cob	1	4.9	174
Fish with batter	1 piece	11.8	216
Hush puppies	3 pieces	1.7	134
Oysters with batter	1 order	13.5	460
Shrimp with batter	6 pieces	8.5	269

	Portion Size	Protein (Grams)	Calories
MCDONALD'S			
Big Mac	1	26	540
Cheeseburger	1	16	300
Egg McMuffin	1	18	350
English muffin (buttered)	1	6	190
Filet-O-Fish	1	14	400
French fries	25	3	210
Hamburger	1	13	260
Hashbrown potatoes	1	1	130
Hotcakes with butter and syrup	1 order	8	470
Pork sausage	1 order	9	180
Pie, apple	1 slice	2	300
cherry	1 slice	2	300
Quarter-pounder	1	26	420
Quarter-pounder with cheese	1	31	520
Scrambled egg	1 order	12	160
Shakes, chocolate	1	11	360
strawberry	1	10	340
vanilla	1	10	320
Sundae, caramel	1	5	280
hot fudge	1	6	290
pineapple	1	4	230
strawberry	1	4	230
PIZZA HUT			
Thin 'N Crispy—10-inch pizza			
beef	1/2 pizza	29	490
cheese	1/2 pizza	25	450
pepperoni	1/2 pizza	23	430
Thick 'N Chewy—10 inch pizza			
beef	1/2 pizza	38	620
cheese	1/2 pizza	34	560
pepperoni	1/2 pizza	31	560
pork	1/2 pizza	36	640
supreme	1/2 pizza	36	640

	Portion Size	Protein (Grams)	Calories
TACO BELL			
Bean burrito	1	11	343
Beef burrito	1	30	466
Beef tostada	1	19	291
Burrito supreme	1	21	457
Pintos 'N Cheese	1	11	168
Taco	1	15	186
Tostada	1	9	179
CHINESE*			
Egg rolls	2	8	260
Barbecued pork ribs	2	12	260
Crispy won ton	2	1	160
Beef chop suey	1 cup	9	180
Chicken Chow mein	1 cup	9	175
Shrimp egg foo yung	1 cup	12	180
Shrimp-fried rice	1 cup	7	200
Pan-fried noodles	1 cup	4	250

---

*Food values computed by the author.

Taste Blindness

Many people who have cancer find that their perception of food flavors changes. This may occur as a side-effect of chemotherapy. It may also occur as a side effect of radiation used to treat malignant tumors of the head, neck, or lung areas, or when cancer of the abdomen or pelvis is treated by radiation. Changing perception of food flavors may also occur as a side-effect of the disease itself. This change is called taste blindness. Some cancer patients who experience it find that even lightly sweetened desserts are suddenly too sweet, or that some protein-rich meats, especially beef, taste bitter. If meats become temporarily unacceptable, try poultry, fish, eggs, or cheese, for taste blindness rarely extends to these.

Taste blindness has also been linked to the aging process. The number of taste buds in one's tongue begins to decrease during middle age. There are four types of taste buds, and each type is individually sensitive to sweet, sour, salt, or bitter. For reasons not yet known, the taste buds that convey sweetness and saltiness decline first. As a result, many older people who do not have cancer discover that once-favorite foods now seem bitter or sour. Thus, when cancer patients who are middle-aged or older experience taste blindness, it may be due to age or to other factors, such as heavy smoking, as much as to anything else.

One way to offset taste blindness is to use more seasonings. Spicy foods just may be the answer. The recipe for Fish Veracruz (page 128) will furnish a clue and so will the recipes for Eggs Rancheros (page 63), Curried Peanuts (page 21), and Pork and Ginger Balls (page 26). A cold glass of Lemonade (page 147) may momentarily spark the ability to enjoy the taste of food. Whatever can be done to make food appealing should be tried in order to improve a shrinking appetite.

Next, try increasing herbs. Or try combining herbs and spices—the best chefs in any country do this as a matter of course.

Other recipes in this book also offer ideas for offsetting taste blindness. Try the Sweet and Sour Pork (page 134), the Mexican Chicken (page 122), and the Baked Green Noodles (page 136). If you find these enjoyable, buy paperback Chinese, Mexican, and Italian cookbooks and try the recipes that call for more seasoning than you would normally use.

Another way to deal with taste blindness is to experiment with the temperatures of food. Cold food, or food at room temperature, may prove more palatable than hot food.

Lastly, when planning a meal, choose foods with good texture and color because texture and color contribute to interest in taste and eating.

Common Problems:
Some Clinical Advice

Enterostomal Surgery (ostomy surgery)

Many cancer patients who have had enterostomal surgery find that certain foods cause discomfort or complications. Highly spiced foods, especially those seasoned with chili peppers, chili powder, cayenne, or black or white pepper, may irritate the area around the stoma. High-fiber raw fruits and vegetables, and popcorn, nuts (including coconut), and coarse whole grain breads can also be abrasive to the area.

Some foods, such as dried beans, cabbage, broccoli, cauliflower, asparagus, and onions, may cause gas and stool odors. Milk, eggs, strong cheeses (such as Roquefort), beer, and carbonated beverages can also create problems.

Two ways to aid digestion: chew foods thoroughly and eat slowly to decrease the chance of swallowing air.

Each person who has had enterostomal surgery has different reactions to various foods; thus, what might be considered a "problem" food for one may not trouble another, and for some there may be no difficulties with any food. The best procedure is to experiment with different "problem" foods to learn how well you tolerate them. Just introduce them gradually, not all in one day.

Swallowing Difficulty

Radiation therapy or surgery to the jaw, mouth, throat, or lungs can cause swallowing problems, and some chemotherapy drugs may cause mouth or esophageal sores that also make swallowing painful. To ease swallowing, try the following:

—Cut any food that can be cut into very small pieces.

—Moisten solid foods with sauces, gravies, butter, or mayonnaise.

—Try a soft diet using cheese and egg recipes or foods with a smooth consistency, such as cream soups, pudding, or yogurt. Soak crackers or toast in milk, tea, or soup. Avoid rough foods, such as raw vegetables, that can scratch the mouth or throat. Purée meats in a blender or try baby food meats and vegetables.

—Try eating foods that are either at room temperature or very cold.

—Citrus fruit juices, ginger ale, tomatoes, or tomato juice may sting your throat. Carbonated soft drinks, grape and apple juice, peach and apricot nectar, bananas, and canned peaches are less acidic and, therefore, less likely to "burn."

—Supplement your diet with instant breakfast drinks to get the extra calories, protein, and nutrients that you need.

—Avoid smoking and drinking—cigarettes and alcohol irritate the mouth and throat.

If swallowing problems persist, ask your doctor for a referral to a speech pathologist, speech therapist, or physical or occupational therapist who knows oral anatomy and is trained to help alleviate swallowing problems.

Weight Gain

Some cancer patients gain weight during therapy, usually because they are taking steroid drugs, such as cortisone or prednisone. These drugs may stimulate appetite to such a degree that excessive weight gain can become a problem. A prudent and well-balanced diet is therefore a necessity. Moreover, since steroid drugs increase water retention, your doctor may suggest a reduction in salt intake, as salt also causes your body to retain excess water. Or, he may choose to prescribe a diuretic, which will increase your body's capacity to excrete fluids.

Diuretics cause loss of potassium, a necessary mineral.* Lost potassium must be replaced daily because a deficiency upsets body fluid balance, causes foot and leg cramps, and leads to muscle weakness and possible damage to the heart muscle. Rich sources of potassium include citrus fruits and juices, prunes and prune juice, tomatoes and tomato juice, pineapple and pineapple juice, bananas, raisins, apricots, potatoes (white or sweet), spinach, meat, fish, chicken, and peanut butter.

Diarrhea

Treatment of tumors in the abdominal region may irritate the intestines and produce diarrhea. Often, raw fruits and vegetables, fried foods, highly spiced foods, dried beans, milk and other dairy products, and beer and carbonated drinks may cause diarrhea.

Foods that may help control diarrhea include bananas, boiled rice or cream of rice cereal, applesauce, and white potatoes—boiled or mashed. Frequent small meals help the digestive process, and it's a good idea to try foods served at room temperature or warm rather than hot (hot foods tend to increase the natural movement of the bowel). Drink fluids between meals instead of with meals, and be sure to include in your diet juices and foods that are potassium-rich. Severe diarrhea can result in the loss of a great deal of potassium and this

---

*Potassium repairs and promotes growth of muscle tissue and regulates cellular water balance.

mineral *must* be replaced daily (see page 208 for suggested food sources).

Sometimes milk or milk products cause diarrhea. Damage to the lining of the intestines resulting from therapy decreases the production of lactase, the enzyme that breaks down the sugar in milk (called lactose). Although lactase deficiency does not interfere with the digestion of most other foods, it can impair the digestion of milk. Ask your doctor about Lact-Aid, available at most drugstores without a prescription. It supplies lactase when added to milk. "Sweet acidophilus" milk, now available in some supermarkets, has a lower amount of lactose than regular milk and may be better tolerated.

Liquid and powdered coffee creamers are lactose-free and can be used over cereal, in coffee, and when cooking. These products have no protein, but *do* contribute calories to your diet. Commercial lactose-free nutritional supplements (like Ensure and Sustacal) can be substituted for milk in puddings, desserts, baked goods, cream soups, and milkshakes. Yogurt or buttermilk may be more easily tolerated because their lactose has been altered in commercial processing.

Constipation

Soft or liquid diets or drugs like codeine and morphine may cause constipation. The following stimulate bowel activity: raw fruits and vegetables; nuts; whole grain breads; cereals; bran or wheat germ added to cereals, cakes, cookies, or milkshakes; dried fruits (raisins, prunes, apricots) and fruit juices; soups; hot tea and hot coffee. A walk or light physical activity after eating may also help relieve constipation. If you think you may need a laxative, stool softener, or occasional enema, be sure to check first with your physician.

NOTE: If your appetite is good but constipation is a problem, six to eight glasses of water daily may be the simplest solution. If your appetite is poor, try to drink caloric fruit juices and other beverages instead of water, which has no calories. If you're losing weight, your priority must be high calories.

IV

MORE HELP

Bibliography

Nutritive Values of American Foods in Common Units. Catherine F. Adams. Agriculture Handbook No. 456, Agriculture Research Service of the United States Department of Agriculture. The most helpful handbook of food values you can own because it lists alphabetically the individual nutritive values of hundreds of foods and ingredients measured in cups, ounces, and can/package sizes. All nutritionists use this book as their basic source of information and refer to it informally as Ag 456. Order from the Superintendent of Documents, U.S. Government Printing Office, Washington, D.C. 20402 (Stock No. 0100-03184). Current price is $5.15.

Laurel's Kitchen: A Handbook for Vegetarian Cookery and Nutrition. Laurel Robertson, Carol Flinders, and Bronwen Godfrey. California: Bantam Books, Nilgiri Press, 1978. The authors give the most detailed explanation of protein complementing available.

Blenderized Diet. Jerry Kukacha. This six-page typescript is available free of charge from the University of Wisconsin Clinical Cancer Center Public Affairs Office, 1900 University Ave., Madison, WI 53705 (telephone: (608) 262-0046). This useful booklet was developed by the author when her husband was recovering from surgery and radiation therapy.

Calorie Guide to Brand Names and Basic Foods. Barbara Kraus. New York: A Signet Book, 1980. A handy reference for the calorie value of supermarket foods.

The Confusing World of Health Foods. HEW publication number (FDA) 79-2108 EV. Marilyn Stephenson. Large type eight-page pamphlet shows some of the nonsensical claims made about natural foods. Free. Write to: Food and Drug Administration, HJF-10, Rockville, Maryland 20857.

Swallowing Problems: Suggestions for Treatment Including Exercises and Diet Modification. Jerilyn Logemann, Ph.D. A new, small, illustrated pamphlet by a specialist in speech pathology and speech therapy. Available from Illinois Cancer Council, 36 South Wabash Ave., Chicago, Il. 60603, for a charge of $1.00.

Cancer Information Services (CIS)

Cancer Information Services (CIS) is a hot line funded by the National Cancer Institute (NCI). CIS offices are in operation nationwide to answer telephone inquiries about cancer and its treatment, and calls are toll-free.

U.S. 24-HOUR NATIONAL NUMBER (use only if no local service number): 1-800-638-6694
ALABAMA: 1-800-292-6201
ALASKA, PUERTO RICO, VIRGIN ISLANDS: 1-800-638-6070
CALIFORNIA: Area codes (213), (714), (805): 1-800-252-9066; Rest of State: (213)-226-2374
COLORADO: 1-800-332-1850
CONNECTICUT: 1-800-922-0824
DELAWARE: 1-800-523-3586
FLORIDA: Dade County: (305) 547-6920; Rest of State: 1-800-432-5953; Spanish-Speaking Residents: 1-800-432-5955
GEORGIA: 1-800-327-7332
HAWAII: Oahu: 536-0111; Other Islands: ask operator for Enterprise 6702
KENTUCKY: 1-800-432-9321; Out-of-State Callers: 1-606-233-6333
ILLINOIS: Chicago: (312) CANCER-1 (226-2371); Rest of State: 1-800-972-0586
MAINE: 1-800-225-7034
MARYLAND: 1-800-492-1444
MASSACHUSETTS: 1-800-952-7420
MINNESOTA: 1-800-582-5262
MONTANA: 1-800-525-0231
NEW HAMPSHIRE: 1-800-225-7034
NEW JERSEY: 1-800-523-3586
NEW MEXICO: 1-800-525-0231
NEW YORK: New York City: (212) 794-7982; Rest of State: 1-800-462-7255
NORTH CAROLINA: Durham County: (919) 684-2230; Rest of State: 1-800-672-0943
NORTH DAKOTA: 1-800-328-5188
OHIO: 1-800-282-6522
PENNSYLVANIA: 1-800-822-3963
SOUTH DAKOTA: 1-800-328-5188
TEXAS: Houston: (713) 792-3245; Rest of State: 1-800-392-2040
VERMONT: 1-800-225-7034
WASHINGTON, D.C., METROPOLITAN AREA: (202) 636-5700

WASHINGTON STATE: Seattle: (206) 284-7263; Rest of State:
  1-800-552-7212
WISCONSIN: 1-800-362-8038
WYOMING: 1-800-525-0231

**Other Information sources using National Cancer Institute
materials:**

KANSAS: Mid-America Cancer Center
          University of Kansas Medical School
          39 Rainbow Boulevard
          Kansas City, Kansas
          (913) 588-4720
OHIO: Ohio State University
        Comprehensive Cancer Center
        Cancer Information Services
        Hamilton Hall 101A
        1645 Neil Avenue
        Columbus, Ohio 43210
        (614) 422-5022

INDEX

scrambled, xi, 62; soufflé, 68, 69;
western omelet, 65; with cream
cheese, 62; zabaglione, 171
Empanadas, meat, 41
Enriched coffee cake, 170
Enterostomal surgery, foods to
avoid, 208
Exercise, 119

F
Fats and oils, 191-92
Fettuccine Alfredo, 138
Fish, Arthur Treacher's Fish &
Chips, 202; as protein source,
140, 190; broiled, 127; Long John
Silver's, 203; nutritional value of,
140, 190; salmon loaf, 129; sauce,
110-12; taste of, 59; Veracruz,
128, 206; whitefish, baked, 119,
126
Fondue, Swiss cheese, 15
Frankfurters, deviled, 45
Freedom in food choice, ix, xi
French toast, 29, 33, 193
Fricassee, chicken, 120
Fried rice, 39
Frittata, 64
Fruit: apples, baked, 164; apple-
sauce, 161; bananas, sautéed,
157; berries and cream, 158; fruit
coupe, 159; grapefruit, broiled,
162; nutritional value of, 191,
200-01; pears, poached, 165;
cinnamon-orange prunes, 160.
See also Beverages, Desserts,
and specific fruit headings

G
German almond slices, 181
Ginger root, 26
Gingersnaps, 180
Gnocchi, ricotta, 42
Goulash, 130

Grapefruit, broiled, 162; with
rum, 162
Greek lemon soup, 95
Guacamole, 14

H
Ham and egg sandwich, 51
Hamburgers, 132, 202, 203, 204
Hash, turkey or chicken, 125
Herb-blend beer bread, 77
Herbed cheese pretzels, 24
Herbed cottage cheese, 72
Herbed lemon sauce, 110
Herbs: for taste, 206; listing of,
141-43; where to order, 143
Hommus, 13
Horseradish cream, 114
Hungarian goulash, 130

I
Information about cancer, sources
of, 213-14
Iron, 189, 190, 191
Italian fruit torte, 174

J
Juices: apricot flip, 152; as antinausea aid, 3; calorie value,
198-99; lemonade, 147; orange-
banana, 150; orange crush, 149;
peach flip, 152. See also
Beverages

K
Kentucky Fried Chicken, 203
Kugel, 37, 193

L
Lactose deficiency, 209
Lactose-free products, 209
Lemon: ice, 163; lemonade, 147,
206; pickled, 117; pound cake,
173; slush, 148; soup, 95;
squares, 167

cream cheese, 55; chicken, 46; cream cheese and olive, 56; cream cheese and strawberry jam, 57; ham and egg, 51; peanut butter, 58; roast beef, 50; sardine, 53; shrimp, 52; Swiss cheese, 54

Sardine sandwich, 53

Sauces, 107-17, 118; cheese, 108; hamburger, 132; hollandaise, 109; horseradish cream, 114; lemon, 110; pesto, 11; remoulade, 112; seafood cocktail, 111; Veracruz, 128; white, 108. See also Spreads and Toppings

Sausage: liver sausage spread, 9; sausage corn muffins, 35

Sautéed bananas, 157

Scallopine, veal, 135

Scrambled eggs with cream cheese, 62

Seafood cocktail sauce, 111

Sesame seeds: sesame crisps, 17; sesame seed dip, 16; sesame seed butter (Tahini), 13

Shakes: apricot flip, 152; banana-yogurt, 151; coconut flip, 146; lemon slush, 148; nutritional value of, 202, 204; orange crush, 149; peach eggnog, 153; peach flip, 152; peanut butter shake, 155; pineapple smoothie, 154. See also Beverages

Shortcake, strawberry, 168-69

Shrimp: salad, 102; sandwich, 52; sauce, 111, 112; tomato-shrimp bisque, 86

Simple berries and cream, 158

Simple spaghetti carbonara, 137

Slush, lemon, 148

Snacks, ix, 6-28; almonds, salted, 20; crisps, sesame, 17; dip, Armenian hommus, 13; dip, Mexican bean, 12; dip, sesame seed, 16; eggs, deviled, 28;

fondue, Swiss cheese, 15; guacamole, 14; meat logs, 27; nachos, 25; nougats, 18; packaged snack foods, 200; pâté chicken liver, 10; peanuts, curried, 21; pesto, 11; popcorn, cheese, 22; pork and ginger balls, 26; pretzels, herbed cheese, 24; spread, beer, 8; spread, crunchy cheese, 7; spread, liver sausage, 9; straws, cheese, 23; trail mix, 19

Sore throat, 145, 207-08

Soufflé, cheese, 68; potato, 69

Soups, 85-96; avocado, 90; canned, 200; consommé, 96; corn chowder, 92; dill, 91; Greek lemon, 95; minestrone, 88; mushroom barley, 87; peanut, 93, 193; potato, 94, 193; tomato-shrimp bisque, 85, 86; vegetable, quick, 89

Spaghetti: carbonara, 137; nutritional value, 191

Sponge cake, 172

Spoonbread, early American, 84

Spreads, 107-17; beer, 8; butter, 116; cheese, 7; guacamole, 14; horseradish cream, 114; liver sausage, 9; mayonnaise, 113

Stove-top rice pudding, 166

Strawberries: and cream, 158; cream topping, 115; jam and cream cheese sandwich, 57; shortcake, 168-69

Stuffed avocado, 102; with crab-meat or shrimp, 102

Stuffed mushroom caps, 43

Sugar cookies, whole wheat, 182

Swallowing difficulty, 207-08

Swedish limpa bread, 78

Sweet and sour pork, 134, 206

Sweet beer bread, 76

Sweet kugel, 37

Sweets: aversion to, 3; desserts,

CANCER DIET/NUTRITION QUESTIONNAIRE

This is a very long questionnaire, but the more help you give us now, the more we will be able to help you in future editions of this book. You need not sign your name. Circle the words that describe your situation and also fill in the blanks. Please detach and return to:

SOMETHING'S GOT TO TASTE GOOD QUESTIONNAIRE
Andrews and McMeel, Inc.
4400 Johnson Drive
Fairway, KS 66205

•••

1. My current treatment is [chemotherapy] [radiation therapy] [both] [neither] [other (specify) _____]. (Circle appropriate answer).

2. Since treatment began:

   2a. my weight has [not changed] [increased by _____ pounds] [decreased by _____ pounds] [fluctuated greatly];

   2b. I [have] [have not] had trouble swallowing. I cannot swallow these foods: _____ ;

   2c. I [have] [have not] had trouble chewing. I cannot chew these foods: _____ ;

   2d. my appetite has [increased] [decreased] [remained the same];

   2e. my appetite for sweets or desserts has [increased] [decreased] [remained the same].

3. Foods I once liked now taste [bland] [metallic] [salty] [bitter] [sour] [sweet] [same as before treatment].

4. The following foods taste especially good now: _____
   _____

5. I now use more of these flavorings/spices: [salt] [pepper] [sugar] [garlic] [onion] [soy sauce] [curry powder] [lemon] [chili powder] [Tabasco sauce] [catsup] [barbecue sauce] [Worcestershire sauce] [mustard] [other (specify) _____].

6. I now use less of these flavorings/spices; [salt] [pepper] [sugar] [garlic] [onion] [soy sauce] [curry powder] [lemon] [chili powder] [Tobasco sauce] [catsup] [barbecue sauce] [Worcestershire sauce] [mustard] [other (specify)_____].

7. I no longer use: [salt] [pepper] [sugar] [garlic] [onion] [soy sauce] [curry powder] [lemon] [chili powder] [Tabasco sauce] [catsup] [barbecue sauce] [Worcestershire sauce] [mustard] [other (specify) _____].

8. I still like: [beef] [pork—roast or chops] [ham] [bacon] [sausage] [veal] [lamb] [chicken] [turkey] [duck] [fish].

9. I no longer enjoy eating: [beef] [pork—roast or chops] [ham] [bacon] [sausage] [veal] [lamb] [chicken] [turkey] [duck] [fish].

10. Food aromas [do] [do not] bother me. If bothered, specify _____

11. I cannot tolerate: [cold foods] [hot foods] [can tolerate either].

12. I cannot tolerate: [cold beverages] [hot beverages] [can tolerate either].

13. I [do] [do not] avoid certain foods/beverages I once enjoyed. (If yes) I now avoid _____ .

14. I [do] [do not] crave a particular food or beverage. (If yes) I crave _____ .

15. To help relieve nausea, I eat, drink, or take: _____ .

16. I [do] [do not] use a nutritional supplement like Ensure, Polycose, or Sustacal. I use _____ .

17. Because I have trouble eating, my doctor [has] [has not] referred me to a nutritionist. If not, why not? _____ .

18. My doctor is [a surgeon] [an internist] [an oncologist] [a hematologist] [a urologist] [a gynecologist] [other (specify)] _____ .

19. The kind of cancer I have is _____ (examples: breast, lung, leukemia, colon).

20. I am being treated at [a doctor's office] [a general hospital/clinic] [a cancer center hospital/clinic].

21. My height is _____ feet, _____ inches.

22. My present weight is _____ pounds.

23. My weight before cancer was _____ pounds.

24. My age is between [10-20] [21-30] [31-40] [41-50] [51-60] [61-70] [71-80] [over 80].

25. I am [male] [female].